Autodesk Inventor Exercises
Learn by Practicing

Design 100 Real-World 3D Models by Practicing

CADArtifex

The premium provider of learning products and solutions
www.cadartifex.com

Autodesk Inventor Exercises - Learn by Practicing
Author: Sandeep Dogra
Email: info@cadartifex.com

Published by
CADArtifex
www.cadartifex.com

Copyright © 2022 CADArtifex

NOTICE TO THE READER

Examination Copies

Electronic Files

Disclaimer

www.cadartifex.com

Dedication

First and foremost, I would like to thank my parents for being a great support throughout my career and while writing this book.

Heartfelt gratitude goes to my wife and my sisters for their patience and endurance in supporting me to take up and successfully accomplish this challenge.

I would also like to acknowledge the efforts of the employees at CADArtifex for their dedication in editing the contents of this book.

Table of Contents

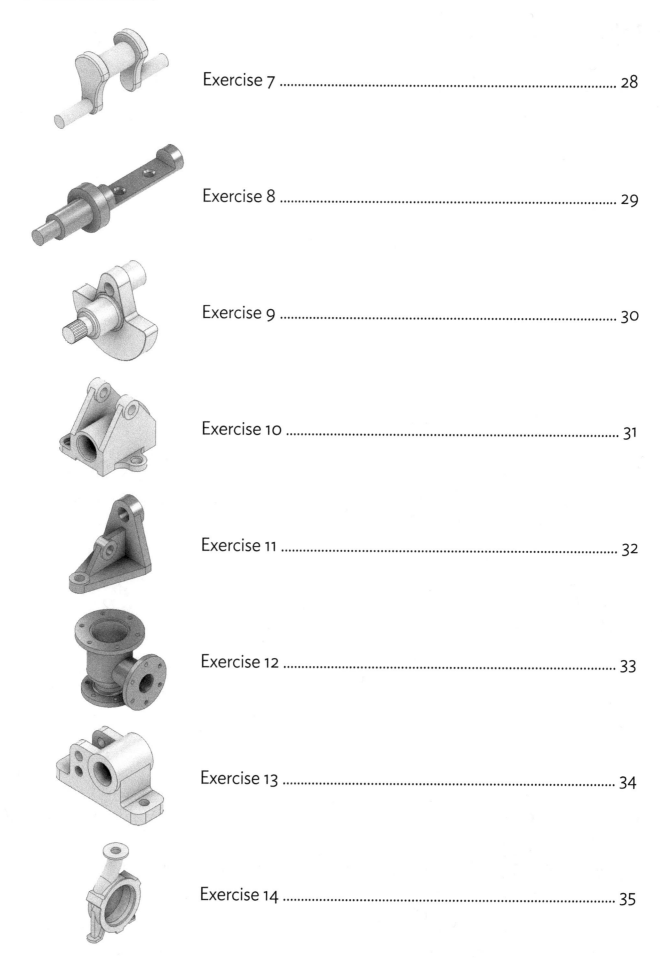

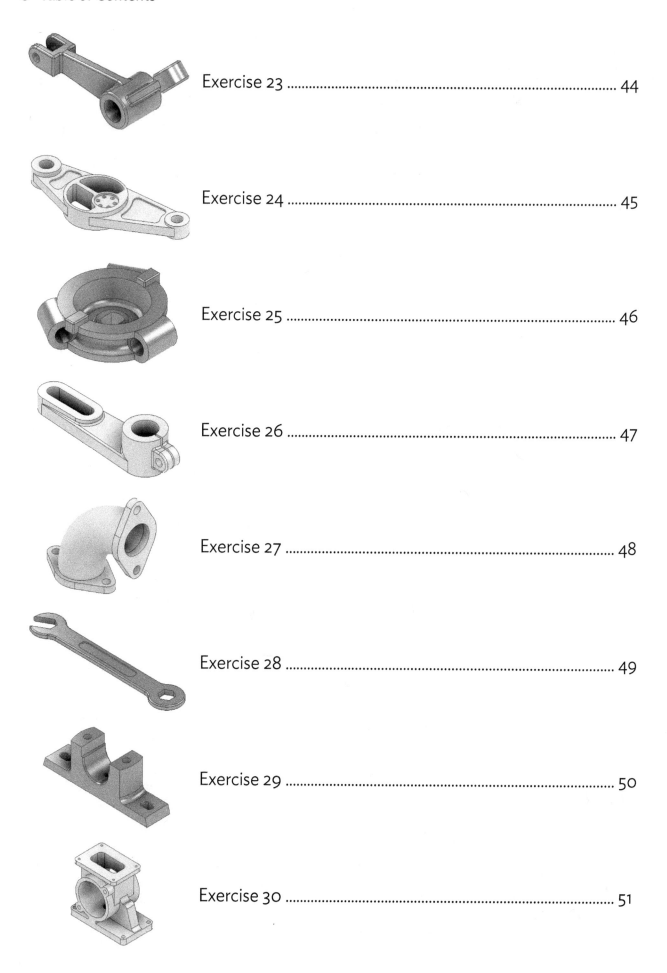

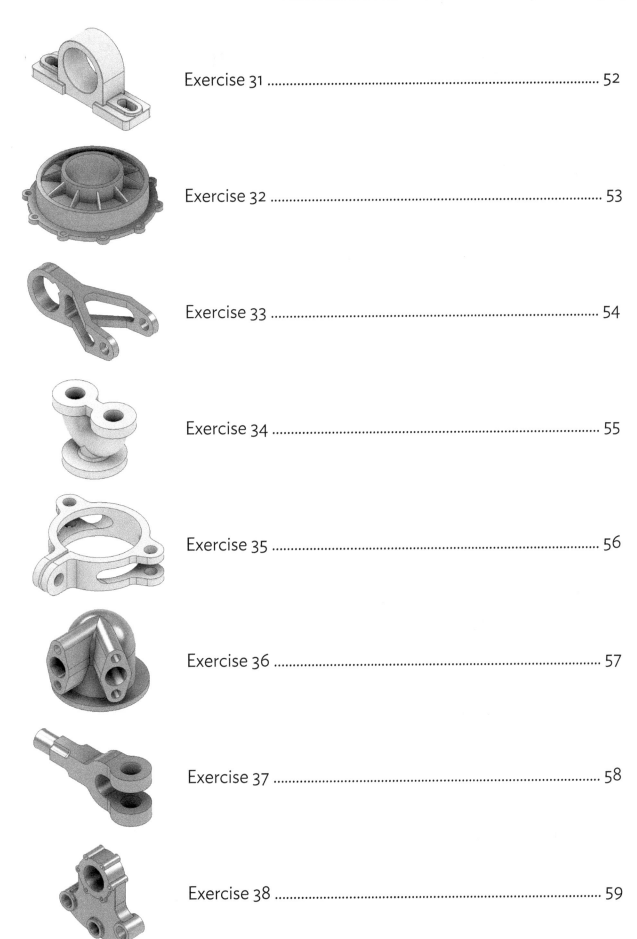

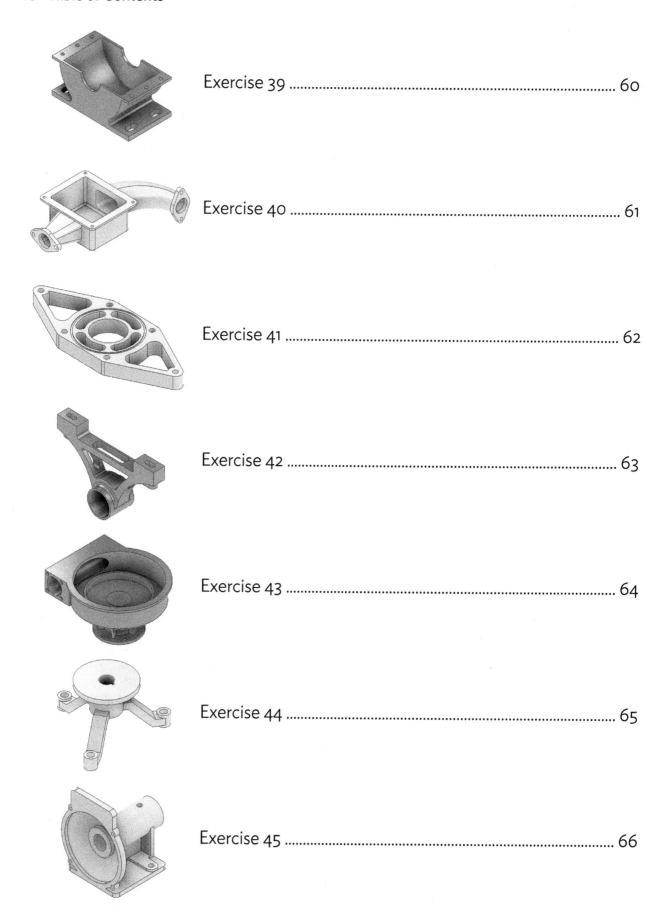

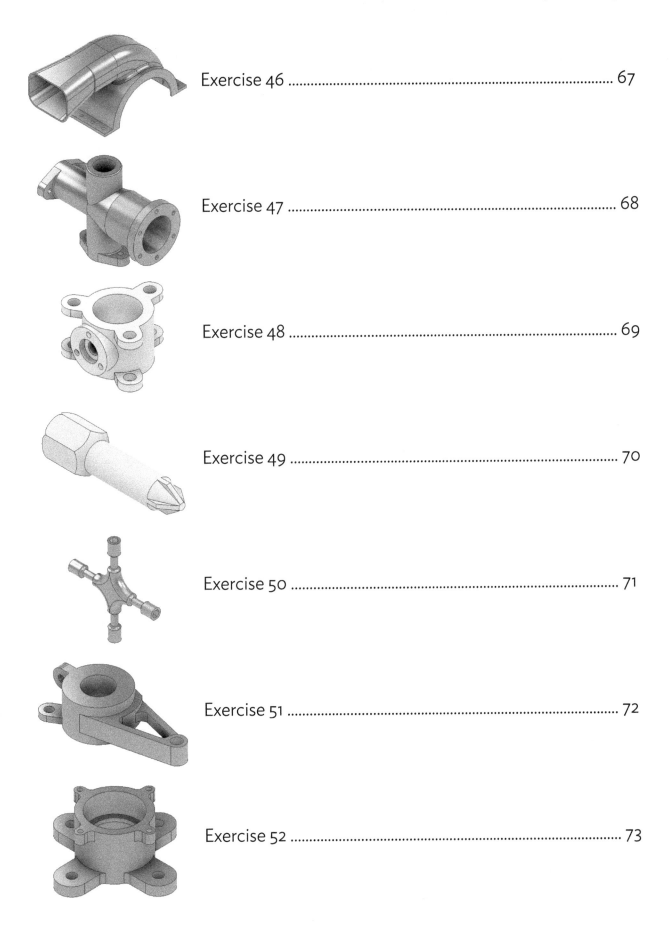

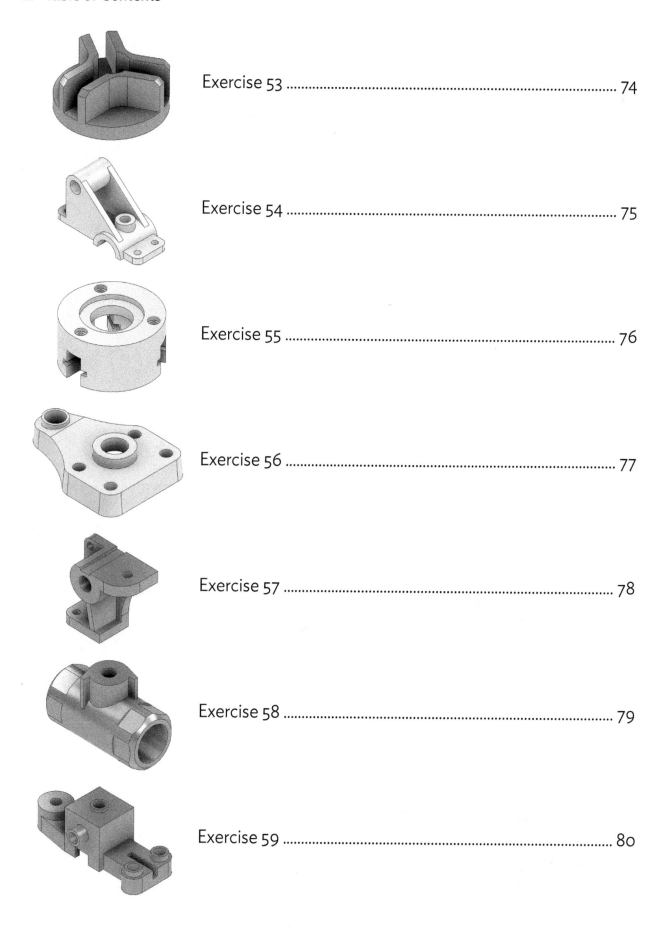

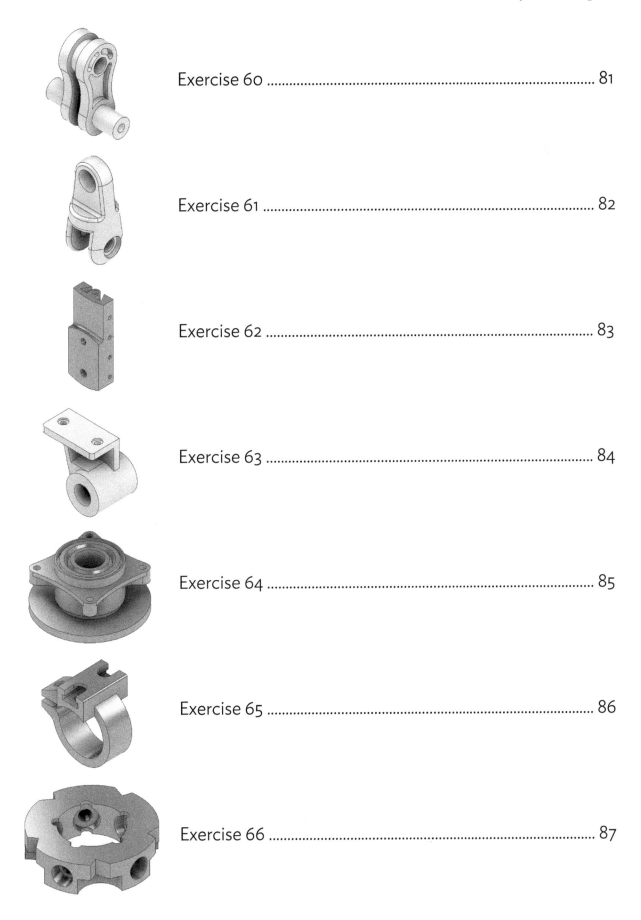

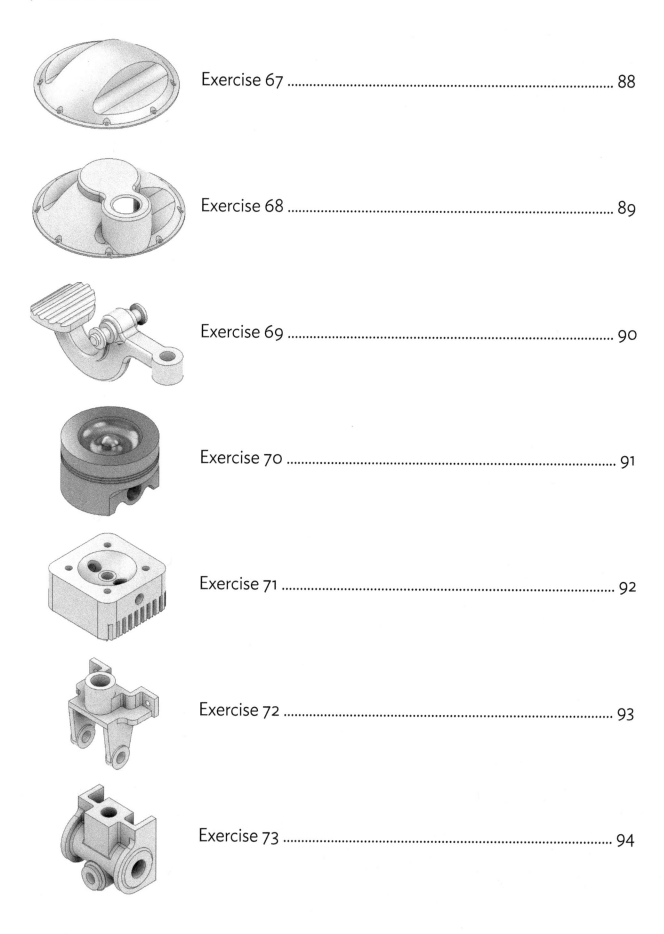

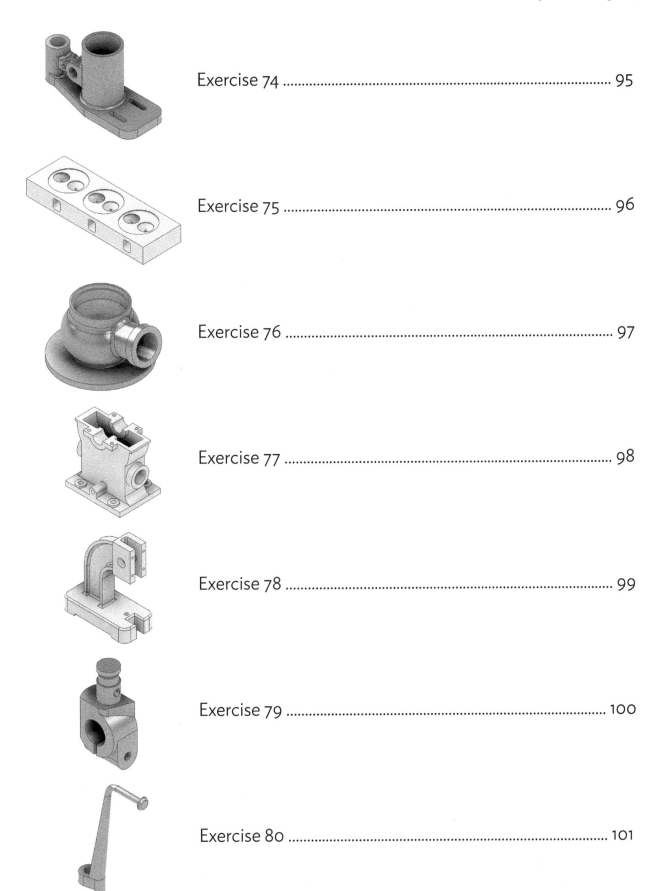

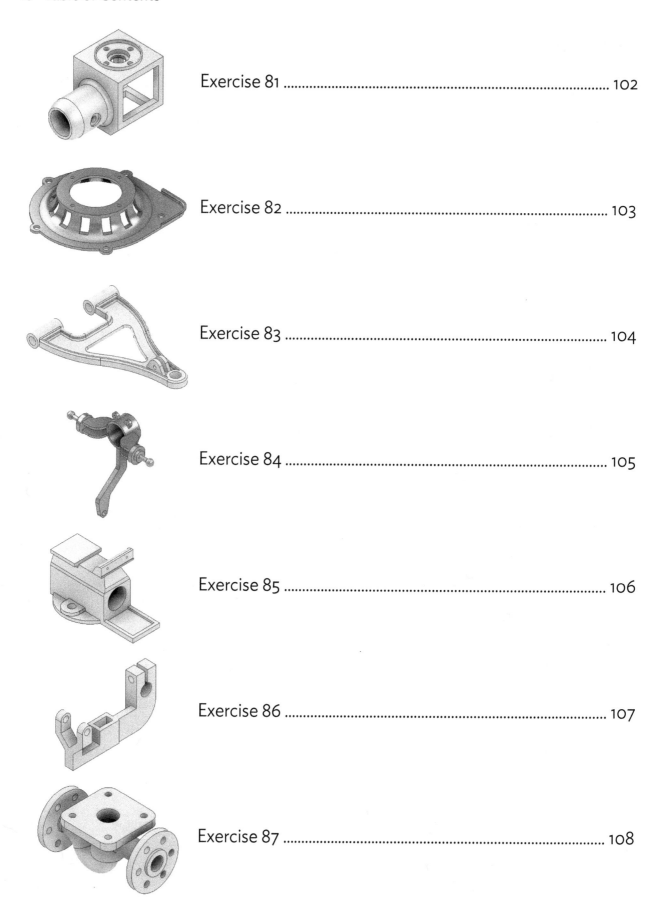

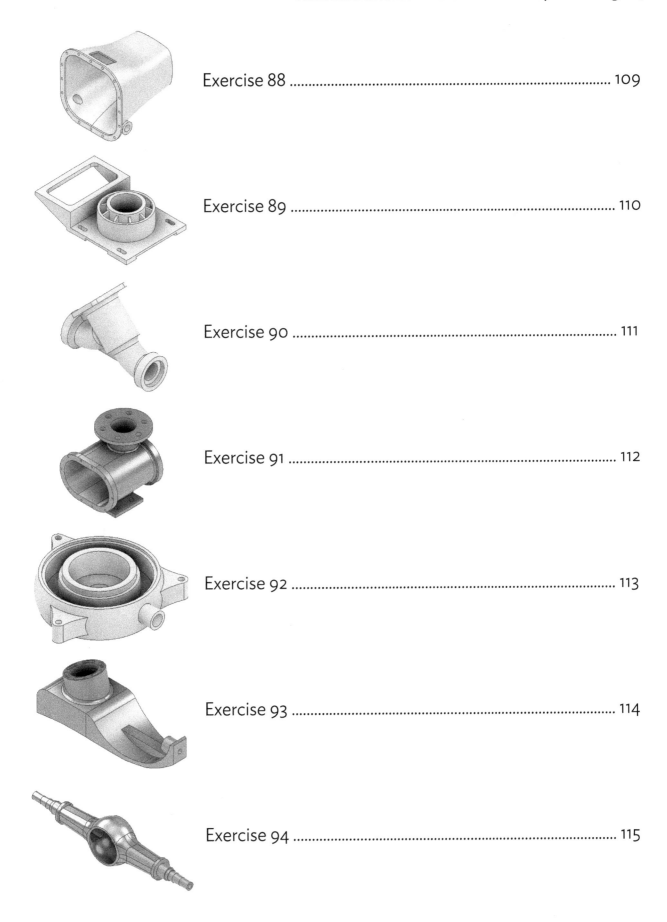

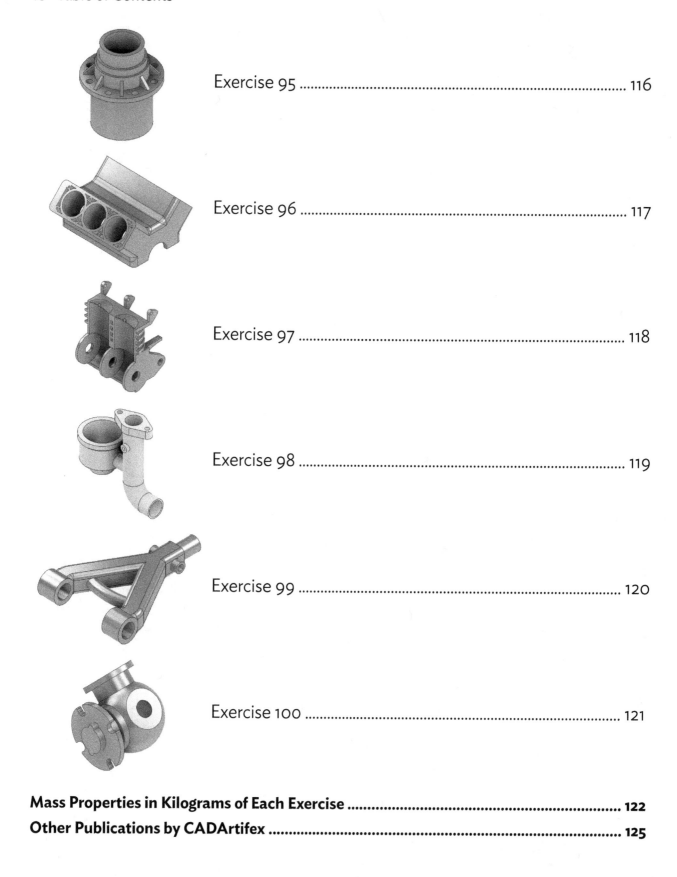

Preface

Autodesk Inventor is a product of Autodesk Inc., one of the biggest technology providers for engineering, architecture, construction, manufacturing, media, and entertainment industries, offering robust software tools that let you design, visualize, simulate, and publish your ideas before they are built or created. Autodesk is a leader in developing software for creators. Moreover, Autodesk continues to develop a comprehensive portfolio of state-of-the-art CAD/CAM/CAE software for global markets.

Autodesk Inventor is a feature-based, parametric solid-modeling mechanical design and automation software that allows you to convert 2D sketches into 3D models by using simple but highly effective modeling tools. Autodesk Inventor provides a wide range of tools that allow you to create real-world components and assemblies. These components and assemblies can be used for generating 2D engineering drawings for production, validating designs by simulating their real-world conditions, visualization, and documentation. It also enables you to create photorealistic renderings, animations, and so on, in addition to creating rapid prototypes of your design. Autodesk Inventor helps in reducing development costs while maximizing efficiency and quality.

Autodesk Inventor Exercises - Learn by Practicing book is designed to help engineers and designers interested in learning Autodesk Inventor by practicing 100 real-world mechanical models. This book does not provide step-by-step instructions to design 3D models, instead, it is a practice book that challenges users to first analyze the drawings and then create the models using the powerful toolset of Autodesk Inventor. This approach helps users to enhance their design skills and take them to the next level.

Who Should Read This Book

This book is written with a wide range of Autodesk Inventor users in mind, varying from beginners to advanced users. In addition to Autodesk Inventor, each exercise of this book can also be designed on any other CAD software such as CATIA, Creo Parametric, NX, SOLIDWORKS, and Solid Edge.

Prerequisites

To complete the exercises given in this book, you should have good knowledge of Autodesk Inventor. If you want to learn Autodesk Inventor step-by-step, you can refer to Autodesk Inventor textbooks published by **CADArtifex**. A list of all textbooks published by CADArtifex is given on the last page of this book.

What Is Covered in This Book

Autodesk Inventor Exercises - Learn by Practicing book consists of 100 real-world mechanical models. After creating these models, you will be able to take your design skills to a professional level.

Downloading Exercises

The exercises used in this book are available for free download. To download the exercises, follow the steps given below:

1. Log in to the CADArtifex website (*cadartifex.com/login*) by using your e-mail id and password. If you are a new user, then you first need to register on the CADArtifex website (*cadartifex.com/register*).

2. After logging in to the website, click on EXERCISES BOOKS > Inventor Exercises > Inventor Exercises - **Learn by Practicing**. The **Exercises** drop-down list appears for downloading the exercises of this book.

How to Contact the Author

We value your feedback and suggestions. Please email us at *info@cadartifex.com*. You can also log on to our website *www.cadartifex.com* to provide your feedback regarding the book as well as download the free learning resources.

We thank you for purchasing *Autodesk Inventor Exercises: Learn by Practicing* book and hope that the exercises given in this book will help you to accomplish your professional goals.

**Inventor
Exercises**

Autodesk Inventor Exercises
Learn by Practicing

(Design 100 Real-World 3D Models by Practicing)

Each of the 100 exercises in the book can be designed separately. No exercise is a prerequisite for another. The drawing views of the exercises given in this book follow the third angle of projection. You can also download each exercise of the book by login to the CADArtifex website (*cadartifex.com/login*) using your login credentials. After login to the CADArtifex website, click on *EXERCISES BOOKS > Inventor Exercises > Inventor Exercises - Learn by Practicing*. If you are a new user, then you need to first register on the CADArtifex website (*cadartifex.com/register*).

Exercise 1.

Create the 3D model, as shown in Figure 1. Different views and dimensions are shown in Figure 2. After creating the model, assign the Stainless Steel AISI 304 material and calculate its mass properties. All dimensions are in mm.

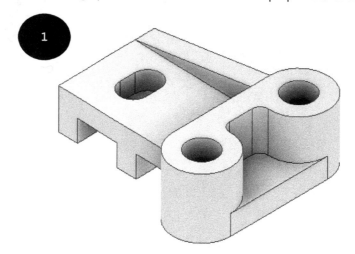

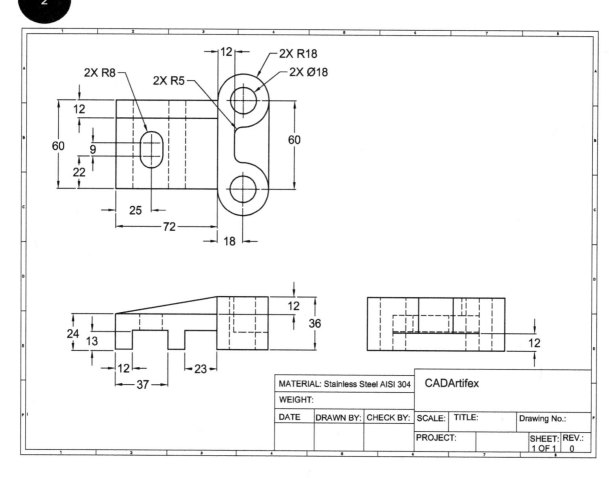

Exercise 2.

Create the 3D model, as shown in Figure 3. Different views and dimensions are shown in Figure 4. After creating the model, assign the Steel AISI 1020 107 HR material and calculate its mass properties. All dimensions are in mm.

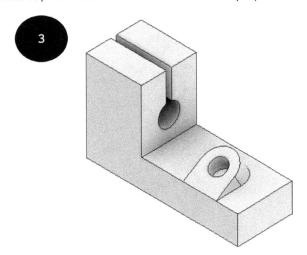

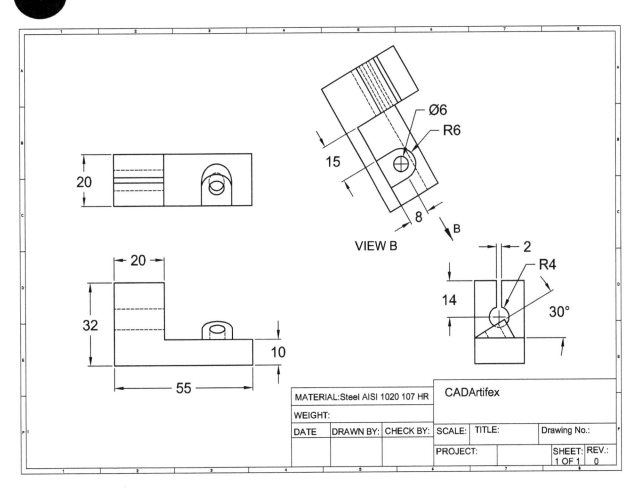

Exercise 3.

Create the 3D model, as shown in Figure 5. Different views of the model and dimensions are shown in Figure 6. After creating the model, assign the Steel, Alloy material and calculate its mass properties. All dimensions are in mm.

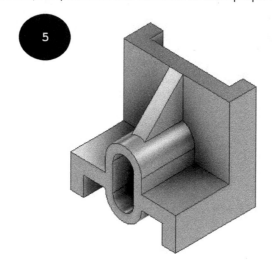

5

6

	5 10
20	

5   2X R4

2X R7

38

10

7

12

30

40

10

14   45°

38

30

MATERIAL:Steel, Alloy	CADArtifex	
WEIGHT:		

DATE	DRAWN BY:	CHECK BY:	SCALE:	TITLE:	Drawing No.:
			PROJECT:		SHEET: 1 OF 1 / REV.: 0

Exercise 4.

Create the 3D model, as shown in Figure 7. Different views of the model and dimensions are shown in Figure 8. After creating the model, assign the Steel, Carbon material and calculate its mass properties. All dimensions are in mm.

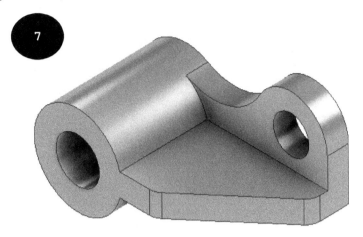

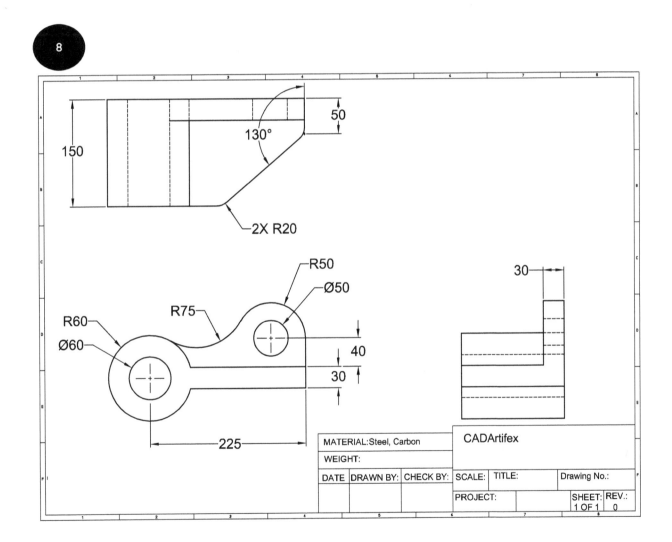

MATERIAL:Steel, Carbon		CADArtifex			
WEIGHT:					
DATE	DRAWN BY:	CHECK BY:	SCALE:	TITLE:	Drawing No.:
			PROJECT:		SHEET: 1 OF 1	REV.: 0

Exercise 5.

Create the 3D model, as shown in Figure 9. Different views of the model and dimensions are shown in Figure 10. After creating the model, assign the Stainless Steel AISI 304 material and calculate its mass properties. All dimensions are in mm.

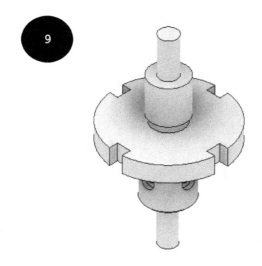

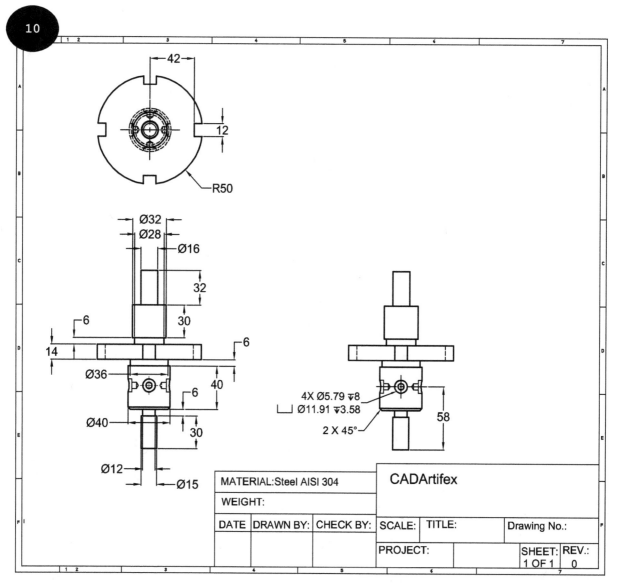

Exercise 6.

Create the 3D model, as shown in Figure 11. Different views of the model and dimensions are shown in Figure 12. After creating the model, assign the Steel, Alloy material and calculate its mass properties. All dimensions are in mm.

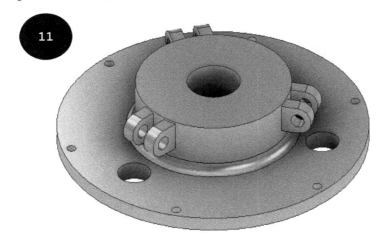

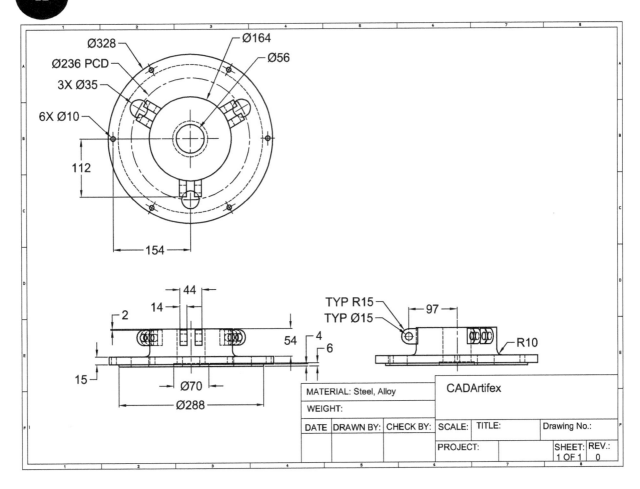

Exercise 7.

Create the 3D model, as shown in Figure 13. Different views of the model and dimensions are shown in Figure 14. After creating the model, assign the Steel AISI 1020 107 HR material and calculate its mass properties. All dimensions are in mm.

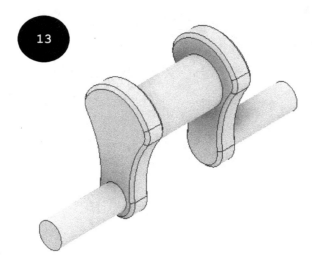

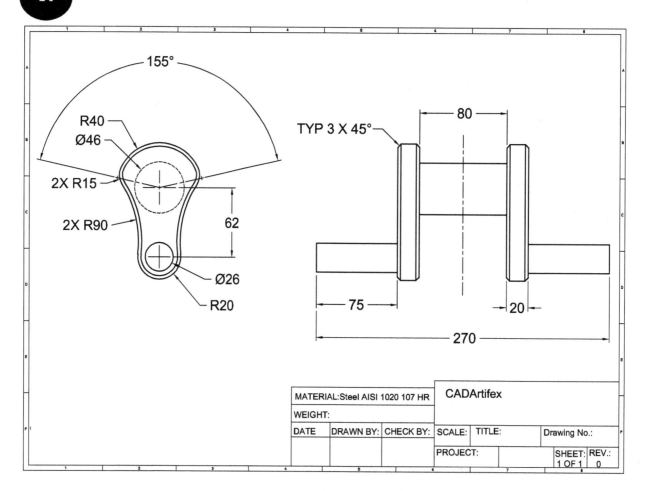

Exercise 8.

Create the 3D model, as shown in Figure 15. Different views of the model and dimensions are shown in Figure 16. After creating the model, assign the Steel, Carbon material and calculate its mass properties. All dimensions are in mm.

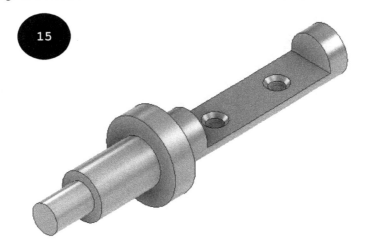

15

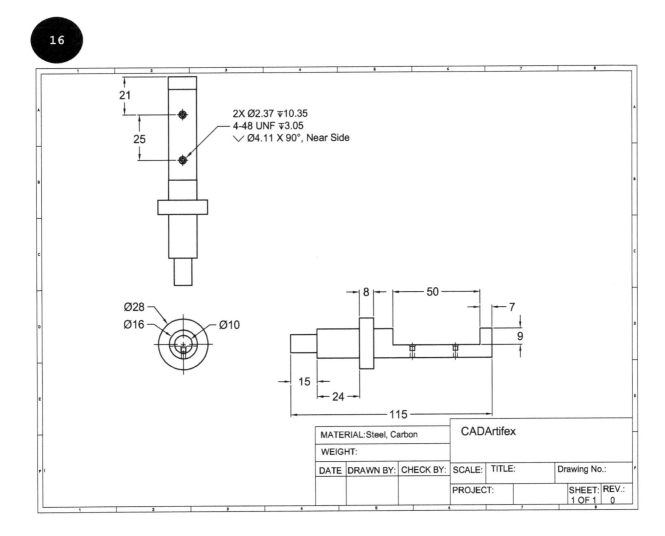

16

21

2X Ø2.37 ⊽10.35
4-48 UNF ⊽3.05
∨ Ø4.11 X 90°, Near Side

25

Ø28
Ø16
Ø10

8
50
7
9

15
24
115

MATERIAL:Steel, Carbon			CADArtifex			
WEIGHT:						
DATE	DRAWN BY:	CHECK BY:	SCALE:	TITLE:	Drawing No.:	
			PROJECT:		SHEET: 1 OF 1	REV.: 0

Exercise 9.

Create the 3D model, as shown in Figure 17. Different views of the model and dimensions are shown in Figure 18. After creating the model, assign the Stainless Steel AISI 304 material and calculate its mass properties. All dimensions are in mm.

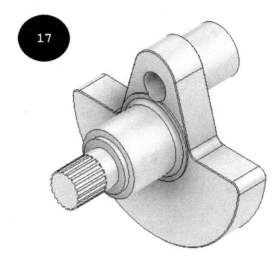

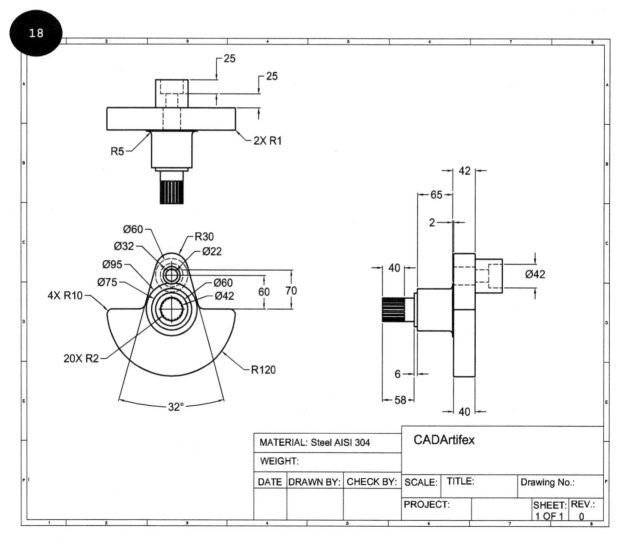

Exercise 10.

Create the 3D model, as shown in Figure 19. Different views of the model and dimensions are shown in Figure 20. After creating the model, assign the Steel AISI 1020 107 HR material and calculate its mass properties. All dimensions are in mm.

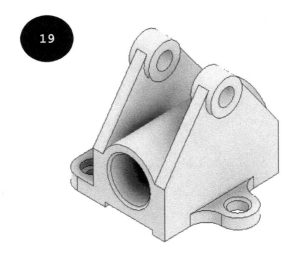

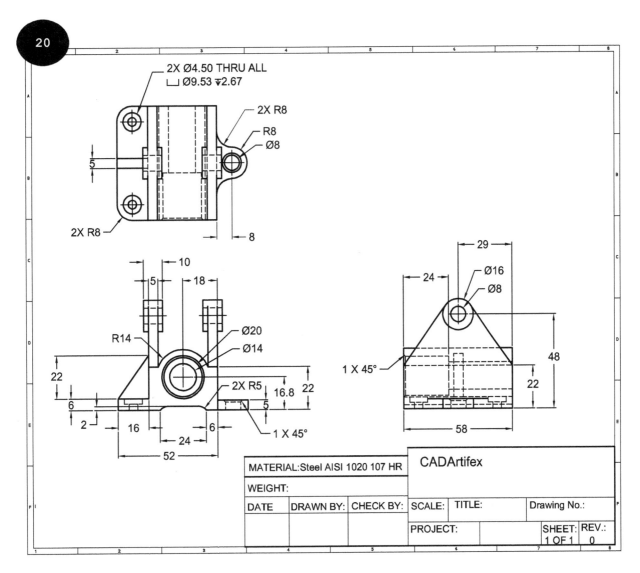

MATERIAL:Steel AISI 1020 107 HR			CADArtifex		
WEIGHT:					
DATE	DRAWN BY:	CHECK BY:	SCALE: TITLE:		Drawing No.:
			PROJECT:		SHEET: REV.: 1 OF 1 0

Exercise 11.

Create the 3D model, as shown in Figure 21. Different views of the model and dimensions are shown in Figure 22. After creating the model, assign the Steel, Alloy material and calculate its mass properties. All dimensions are in mm.

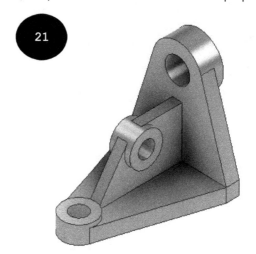

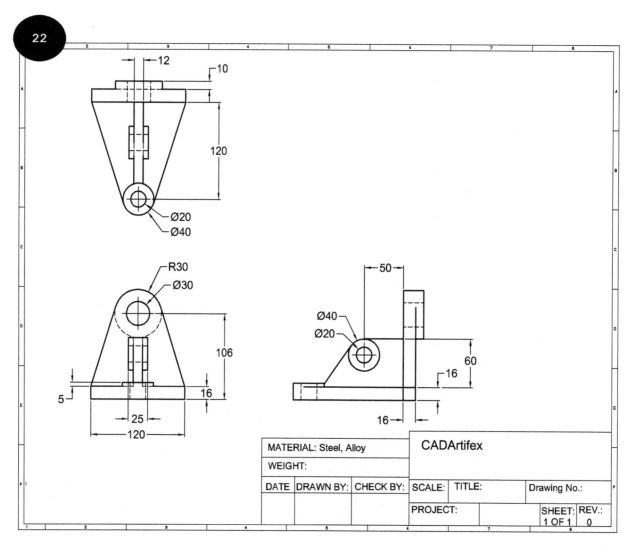

MATERIAL: Steel, Alloy				CADArtifex		
WEIGHT:						
DATE	DRAWN BY:	CHECK BY:	SCALE:	TITLE:	Drawing No.:	
			PROJECT:		SHEET: 1 OF 1	REV.: 0

Exercise 12.

Create the 3D model, as shown in Figure 23. Different views of the model and dimensions are shown in Figure 24. After creating the model, assign the Steel, Carbon material and calculate its mass properties. All dimensions are in mm.

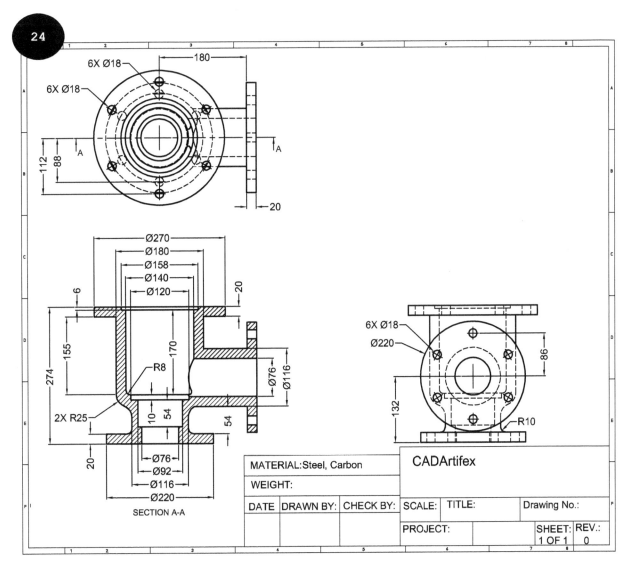

SECTION A-A

MATERIAL:Steel, Carbon			CADArtifex		
WEIGHT:					
DATE	DRAWN BY:	CHECK BY:	SCALE:	TITLE:	Drawing No.:
			PROJECT:		SHEET: 1 OF 1	REV.: 0

Exercise 13.

Create the 3D model, as shown in Figure 25. Different views of the model and dimensions are shown in Figure 26. After creating the model, assign the Stainless Steel AISI 304 material and calculate its mass properties. All dimensions are in mm.

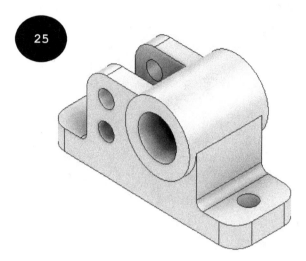

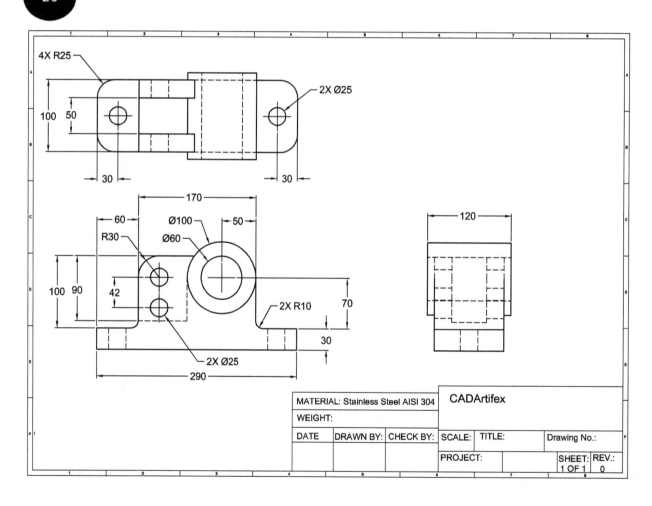

Exercise 14.

Create the 3D model, as shown in Figure 27. Different views of the model and dimensions are shown in Figure 28. After creating the model, assign the Steel AISI 1020 107 HR material and calculate its mass properties. All dimensions are in mm.

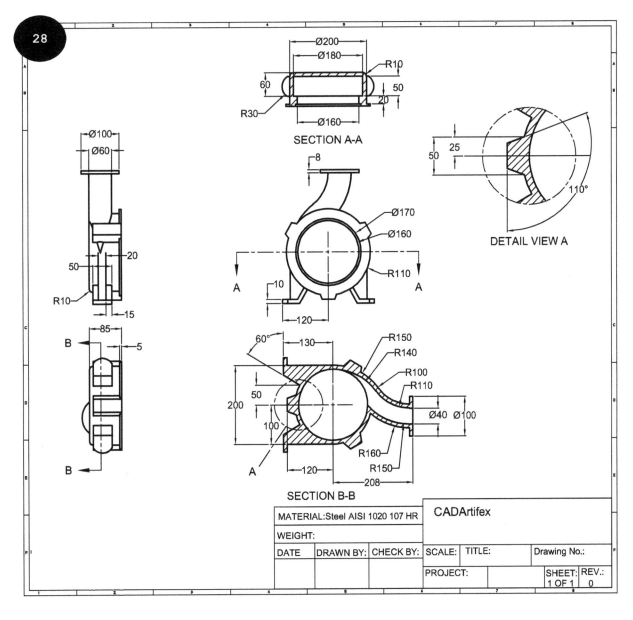

Exercise 15.

Create the 3D model, as shown in Figure 29. Different views of the model and dimensions are shown in Figure 30. After creating the model, assign the Steel, Alloy material and calculate its mass properties. All dimensions are in mm.

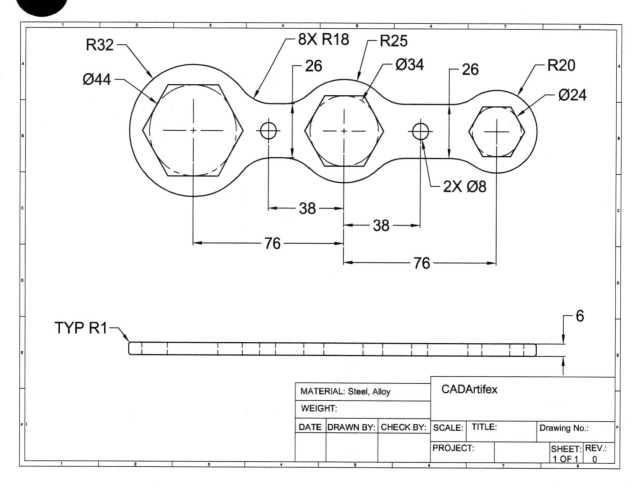

Exercise 16.

Create the 3D model, as shown in Figure 31. Different views of the model and dimensions are shown in Figure 32. After creating the model, assign the Steel, Carbon material and calculate its mass properties. All dimensions are in mm.

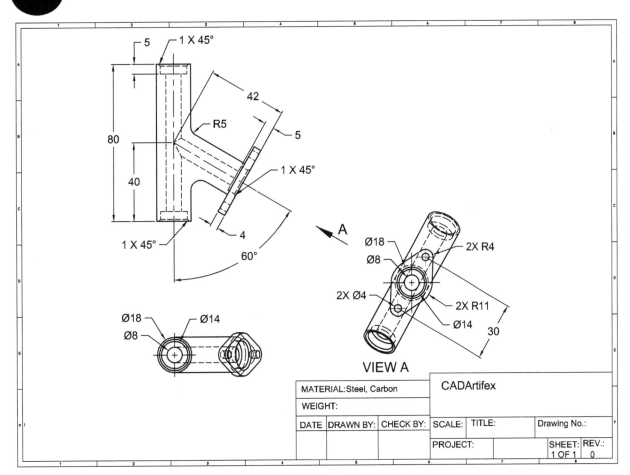

38

Exercise 17.

Create the 3D model, as shown in Figure 33. Different views of the model and dimensions are shown in Figure 34. After creating the model, assign the Stainless Steel AISI 304 material and calculate its mass properties. All dimensions are in mm.

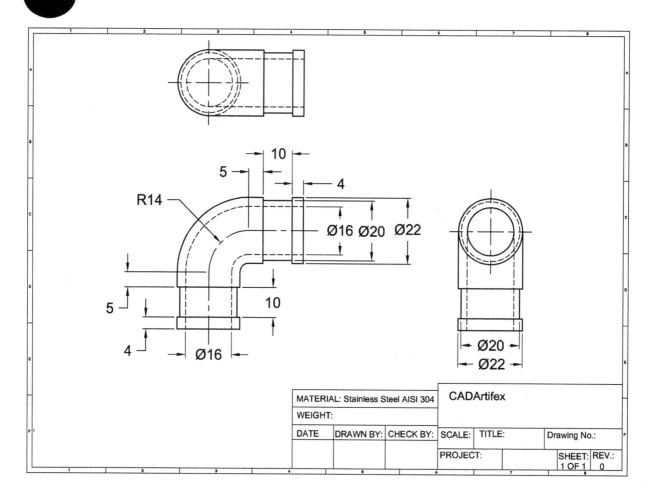

Exercise 18.

Create the 3D model, as shown in Figure 35. Different views of the model and dimensions are shown in Figure 36. After creating the model, assign the Steel AISI 1020 107 HR material and calculate its mass properties. All dimensions are in mm.

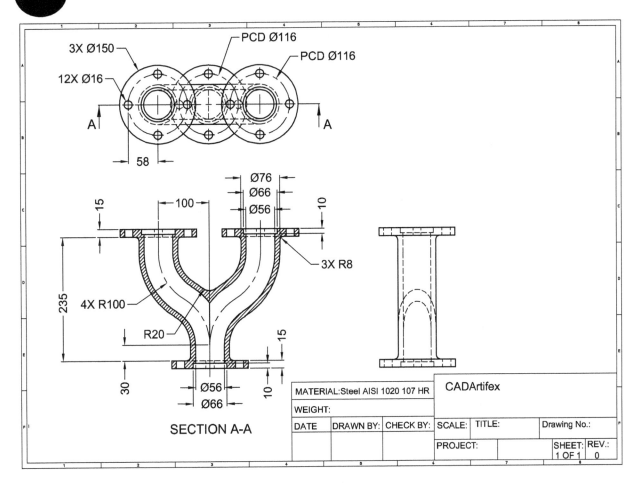

Exercise 19.

Create the 3D model, as shown in Figure 37. Different views of the model and dimensions are shown in Figure 38. After creating the model, assign the Steel, Alloy material and calculate its mass properties. All dimensions are in mm.

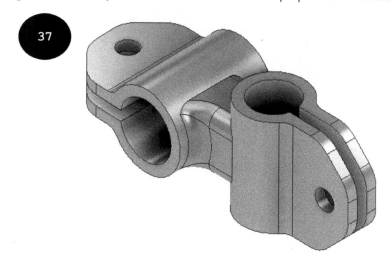

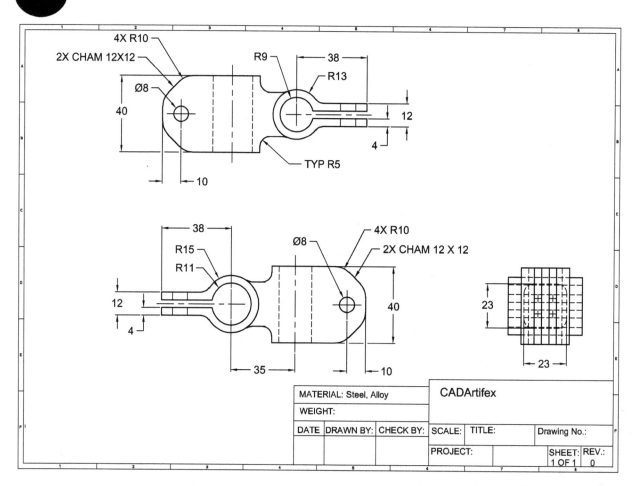

Exercise 20.

Create the 3D model, as shown in Figure 39. Different views of the model and dimensions are shown in Figure 40. After creating the model, assign the Steel, Carbon material and calculate its mass properties. All dimensions are in mm.

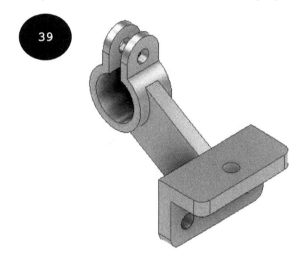

39

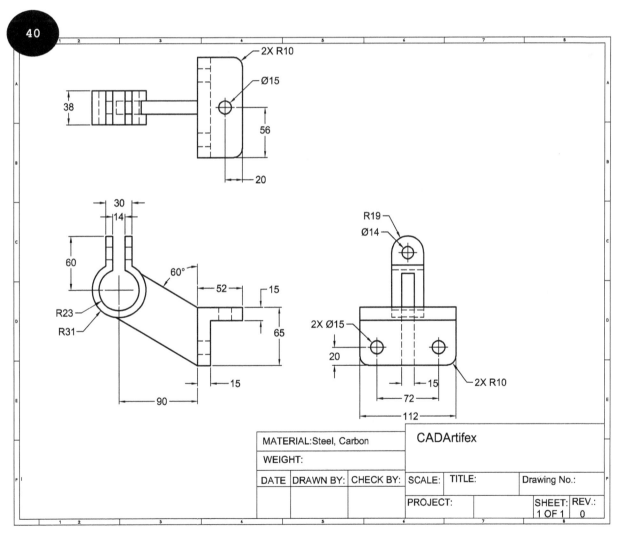

Exercise 21.

Create the 3D model, as shown in Figure 41. Different views of the model and dimensions are shown in Figure 42. After creating the model, assign the Stainless Steel AISI 304 material and calculate its mass properties. All dimensions are in mm.

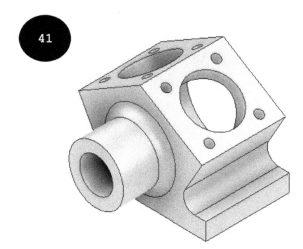

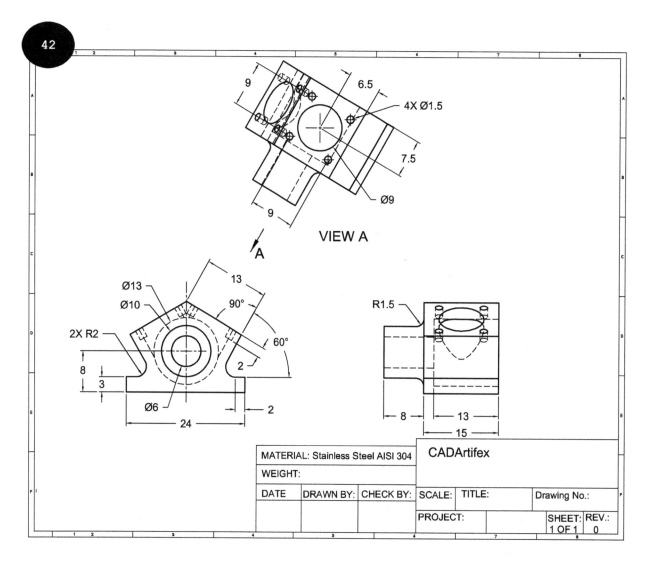

Exercise 22.

Create the 3D model, as shown in Figure 43. Different views of the model and dimensions are shown in Figure 44. After creating the model, assign the Steel AISI 1020 107 HR material and calculate its mass properties. All dimensions are in mm.

43

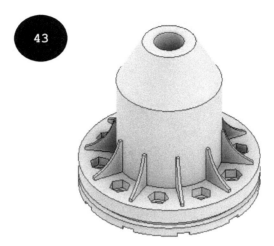

44

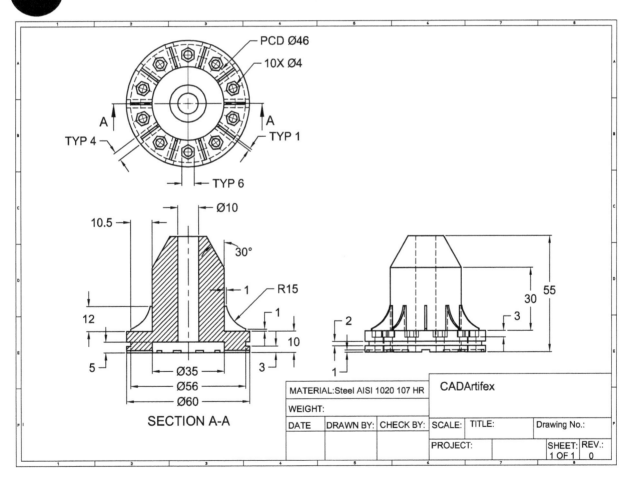

PCD Ø46

10X Ø4

A   A

TYP 4   TYP 1

TYP 6

10.5   Ø10

30°

1   R15

12   1

2   3

5   Ø35   3   10

Ø56

Ø60

30   55

1

SECTION A-A

MATERIAL:Steel AISI 1020 107 HR		CADArtifex		
WEIGHT:				
DATE	DRAWN BY:	CHECK BY:	SCALE:	TITLE:
			PROJECT:	

Exercise 23.

Create the 3D model, as shown in Figure 45. Different views of the model and dimensions are shown in Figure 46. After creating the model, assign the Steel, Alloy material and calculate its mass properties. All dimensions are in mm.

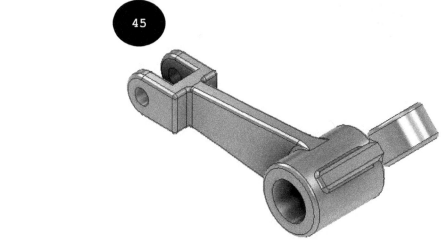

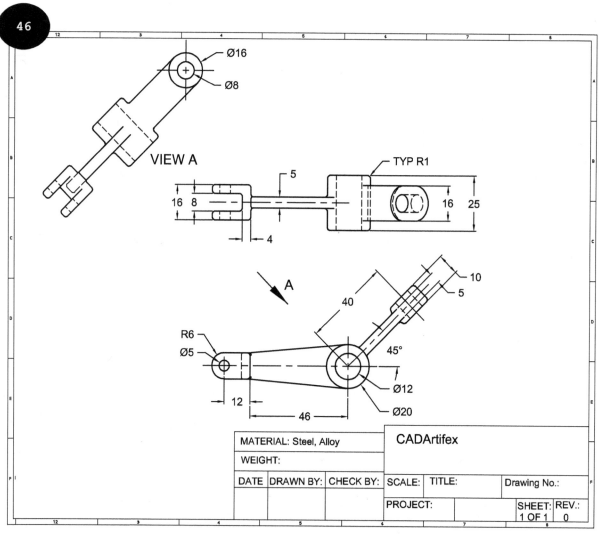

Exercise 24.

Create the 3D model, as shown in Figure 47. Different views of the model and dimensions are shown in Figure 48. After creating the model, assign the Steel AISI 1020 107 HR material and calculate its mass properties. All dimensions are in mm.

47

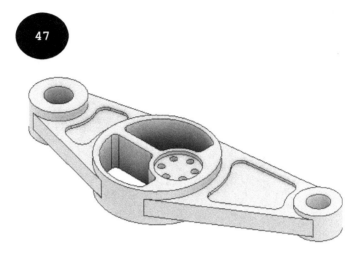

48

Exercise 25.

Create the 3D model, as shown in Figure 49. Different views of the model and dimensions are shown in Figure 50. After creating the model, assign the Steel, Alloy material and calculate its mass properties. All dimensions are in mm.

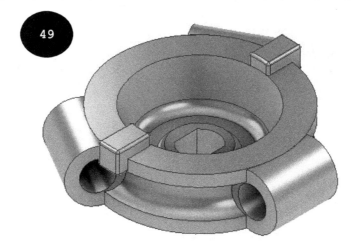

49

50

20

2X R18

92

28

A   A

60

Ø50

24

R25

Ø28

38

74°

R14

5

25

10

Ø56

6

Ø124

R10

Ø166

SECTION A-A

R5   TYP R2   10

21

4X R2

MATERIAL: Steel, Alloy		CADArtifex		
WEIGHT:				
DATE	DRAWN BY:	CHECK BY:	SCALE:	TITLE:	Drawing No.:
			PROJECT:		SHEET: 1 OF 1	REV.: 0

Exercise 26.

Create the 3D model, as shown in Figure 51. Different views of the model and dimensions are shown in Figure 52. After creating the model, assign the Stainless Steel AISI 304 material and calculate its mass properties. All dimensions are in mm.

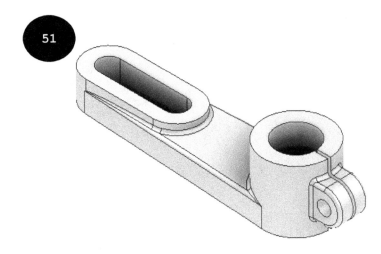

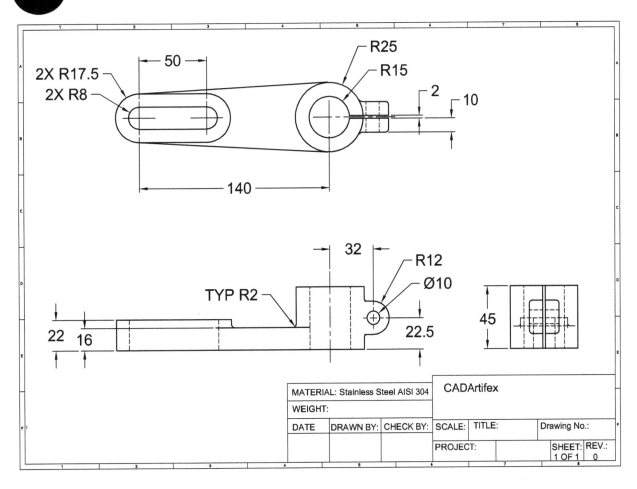

Exercise 27.

Create the 3D model, as shown in Figure 53. Different views of the model and dimensions are shown in Figure 54. After creating the model, assign the Steel AISI 1020 107 HR material and calculate its mass properties. All dimensions are in mm.

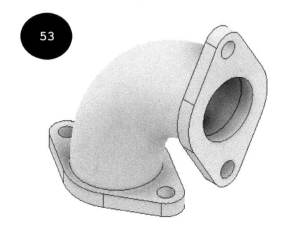

53

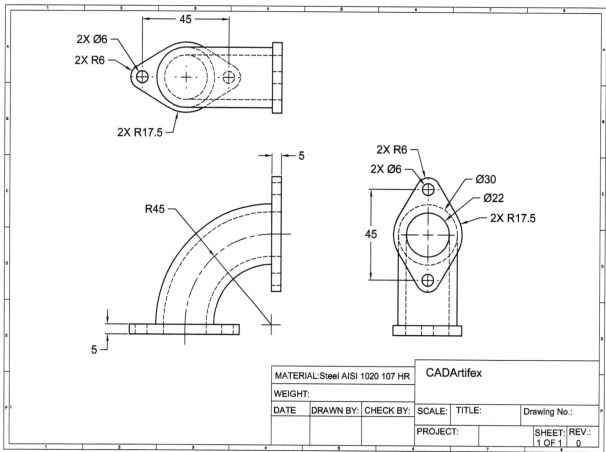

54

Exercise 28.

Create the 3D model, as shown in Figure 55. Different views of the model and dimensions are shown in Figure 56. After creating the model, assign the Steel, Alloy material and calculate its mass properties. All dimensions are in mm.

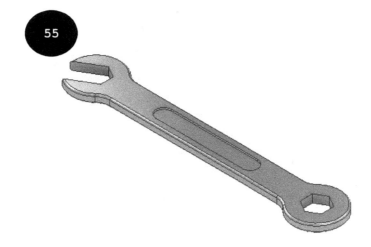

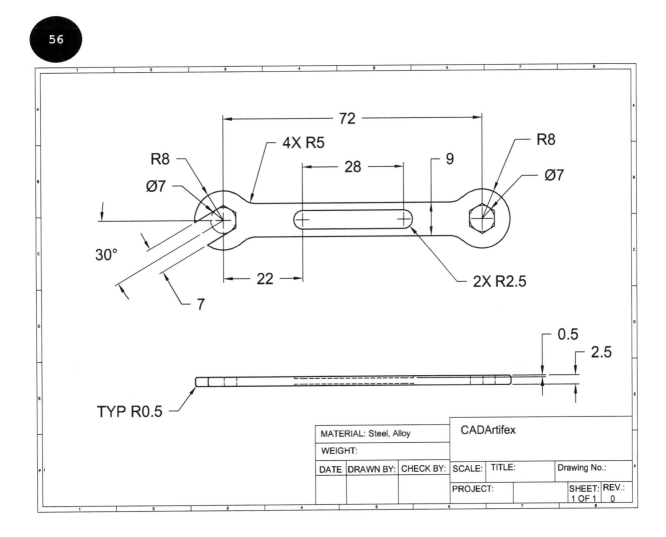

Exercise 29.

Create the 3D model, as shown in Figure 57. Different views of the model and dimensions are shown in Figure 58. After creating the model, assign the Steel, Carbon Steel material and calculate its mass properties. All dimensions are in mm.

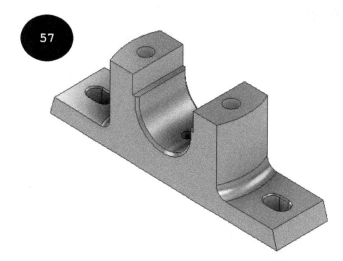

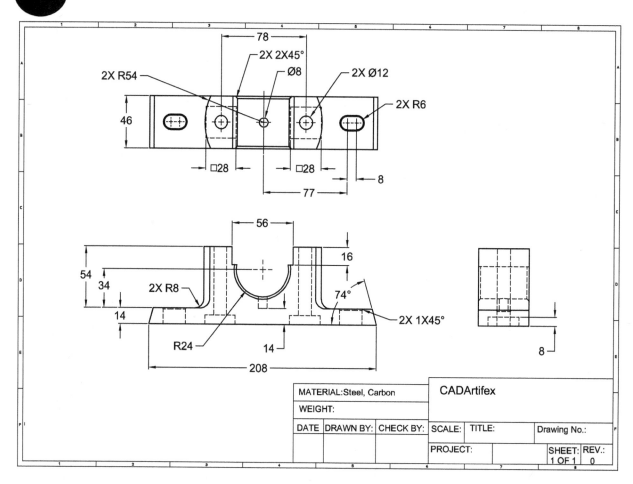

Exercise 30.

Create the 3D model, as shown in Figure 59. Different views of the model and dimensions are shown in Figure 60. After creating the model, assign the Stainless Steel AISI 304 material and calculate its mass properties. All dimensions are in mm.

59

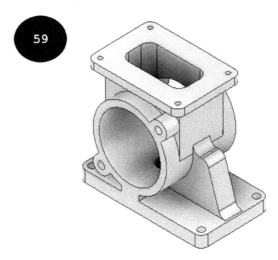

60

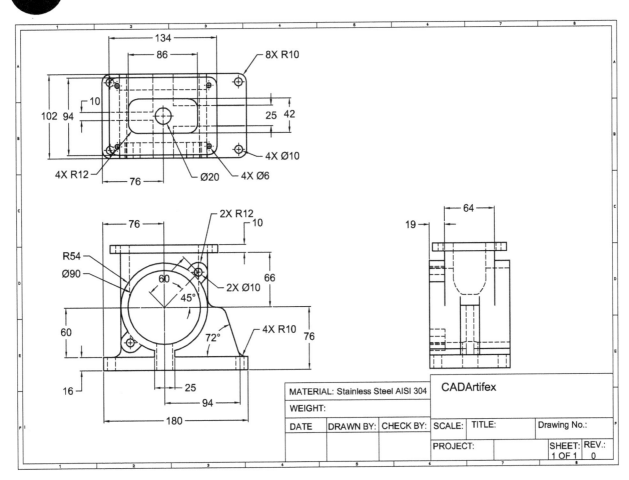

Exercise 31.

Create the 3D model, as shown in Figure 61. Different views of the model and dimensions are shown in Figure 62. After creating the model, assign the Steel AISI 1020 107 HR material and calculate its mass properties. All dimensions are in mm.

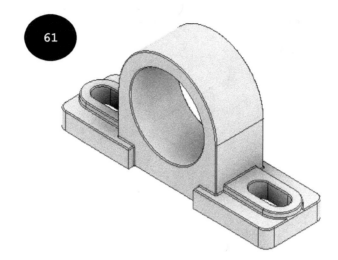

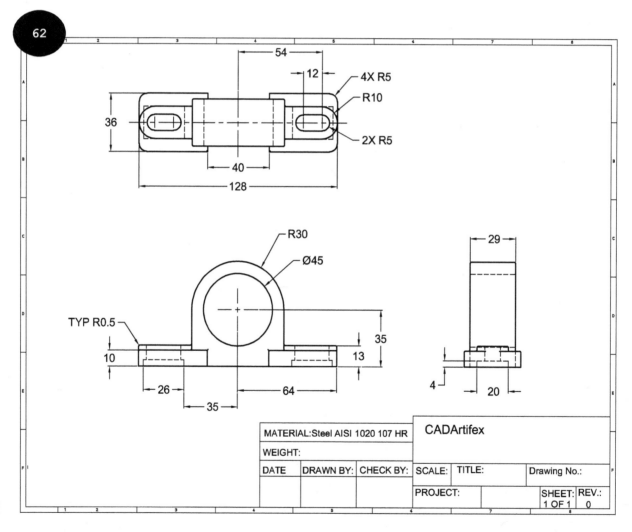

Exercise 32.

Create the 3D model, as shown in Figure 63. Different views of the model and dimensions are shown in Figure 64. After creating the model, assign the Steel, Alloy material and calculate its mass properties. All dimensions are in mm.

63

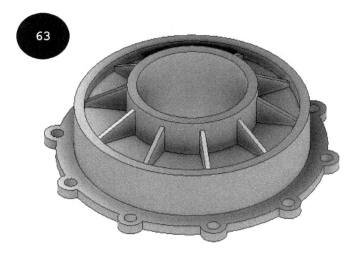

64

10X Ø8

10X R8

R83

3

5

3

6

3

50

35

22

6

Ø68

Ø80

Ø132

Ø144

Ø166

3

SECTION A-A

MATERIAL: Steel, Alloy			CADArtifex			
WEIGHT:						
DATE	DRAWN BY:	CHECK BY:	SCALE:	TITLE:		Drawing No.:
			PROJECT:			SHEET: REV.: 1 OF 1 0

Exercise 33.

Create the 3D model, as shown in Figure 65. Different views of the model and dimensions are shown in Figure 66. After creating the model, assign the Steel, Carbon material and calculate its mass properties. All dimensions are in mm.

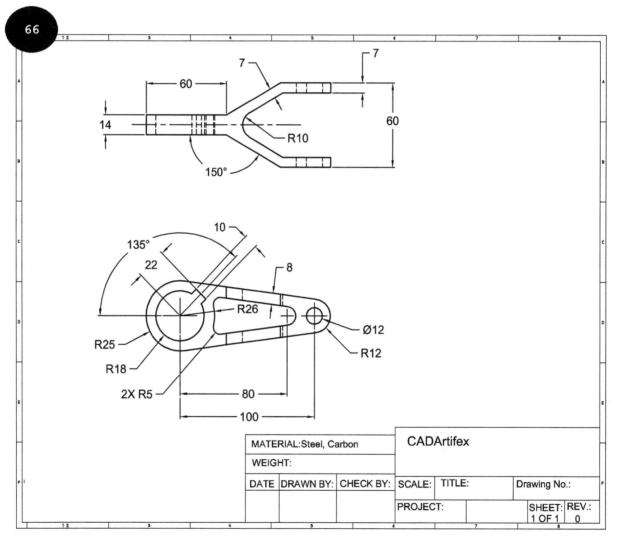

MATERIAL:Steel, Carbon			CADArtifex			
WEIGHT:						
DATE	DRAWN BY:	CHECK BY:	SCALE:	TITLE:		Drawing No.:
			PROJECT:			SHEET: 1 OF 1	REV.: 0

Exercise 34.

Create the 3D model, as shown in Figure 67. Different views of the model and dimensions are shown in Figure 68. After creating the model, assign the Stainless Steel AISI 304 material and calculate its mass properties. All dimensions are in mm.

67

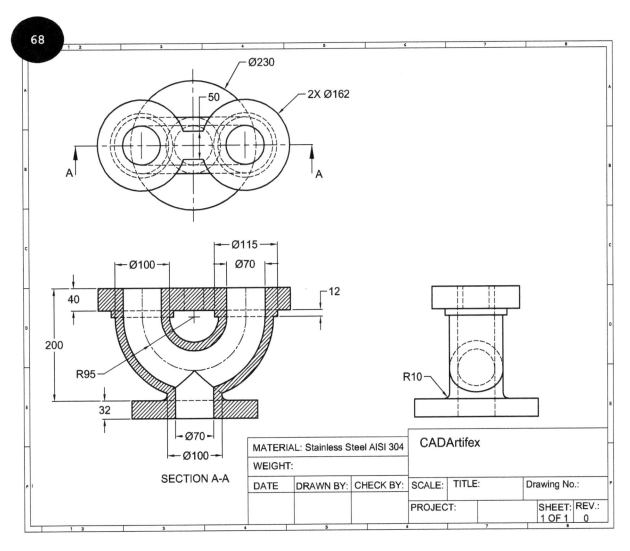

68

Exercise 35.

Create the 3D model, as shown in Figure 69. Different views of the model and dimensions are shown in Figure 70. After creating the model, assign the Steel AISI 1020 107 HR material and calculate its mass properties. All dimensions are in mm.

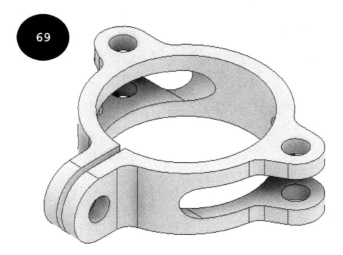

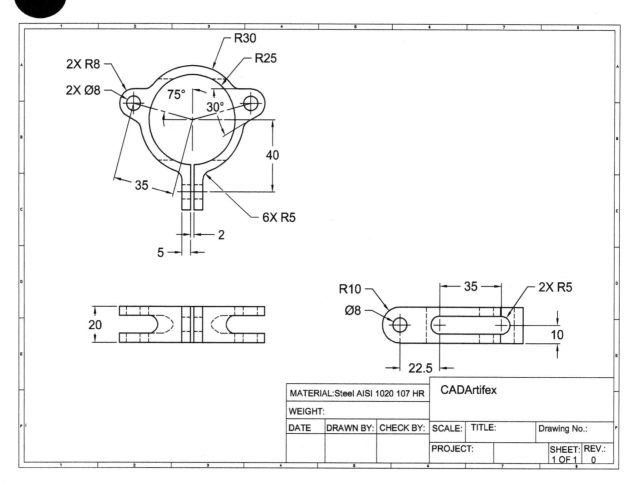

Exercise 36.

Create the 3D model, as shown in Figure 71. Different views of the model and dimensions are shown in Figure 72. After creating the model, assign the Steel, Alloy material and calculate its mass properties. All dimensions are in mm.

71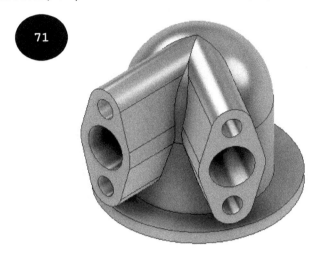

72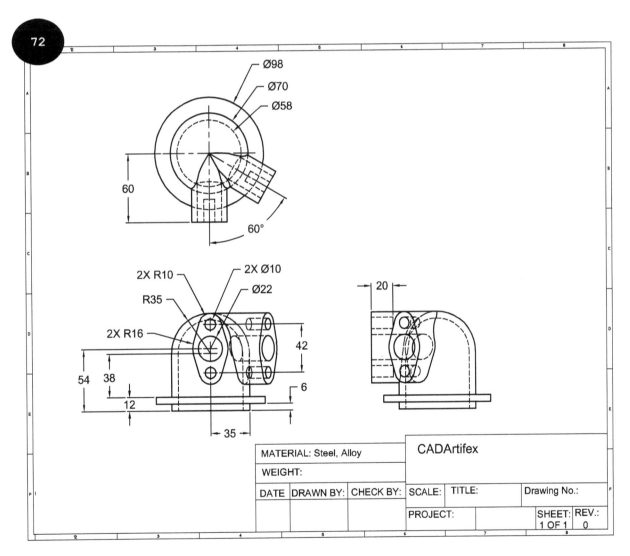

Exercise 37.

Create the 3D model, as shown in Figure 73. Different views of the model and dimensions are shown in Figure 74. After creating the model, assign the Steel, Carbon material and calculate its mass properties. All dimensions are in mm.

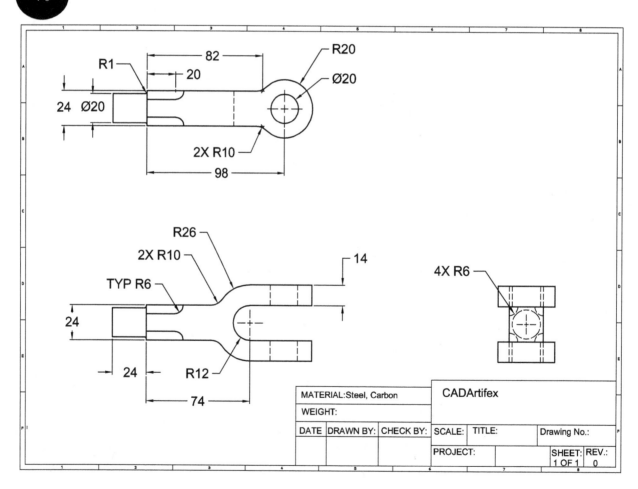

Exercise 38.

Create the 3D model, as shown in Figure 75. Different views of the model and dimensions are shown in Figure 76. After creating the model, assign the Steel, Alloy material and calculate its mass properties. All dimensions are in mm.

75

76

6X Ø6

R31

6X R6

Ø40

3X Ø20

2X R18

3X Ø30

80°

R85

R100

32

22

TYP R1

32

MATERIAL: Steel, Alloy			CADArtifex		
WEIGHT:					
DATE	DRAWN BY:	CHECK BY:	SCALE:	TITLE:	Drawing No.:
			PROJECT:		SHEET: 1 OF 1 / REV.: 0

Exercise 39.

Create the 3D model, as shown in Figure 77. Different views of the model and dimensions are shown in Figure 78. After creating the model, assign the Steel, Carbon material and calculate its mass properties. All dimensions are in mm.

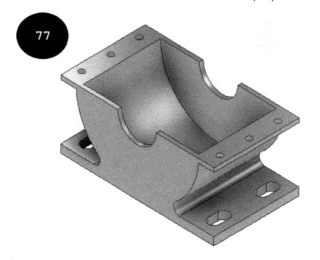

77

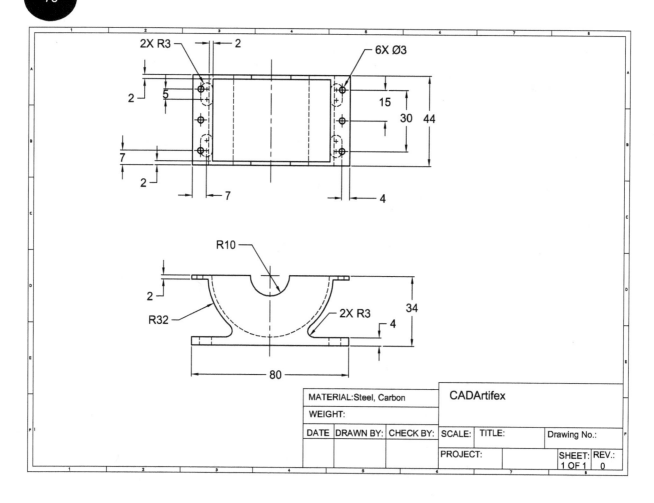

78

Exercise 40.

Create the 3D model, as shown in Figure 79. Different views of the model and dimensions are shown in Figure 80. After creating the model, assign the Stainless Steel AISI 304 material and calculate its mass properties. All dimensions are in mm.

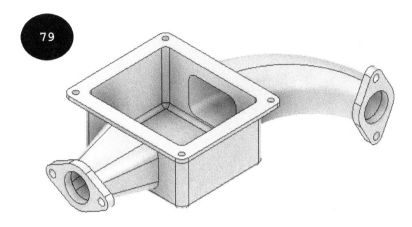

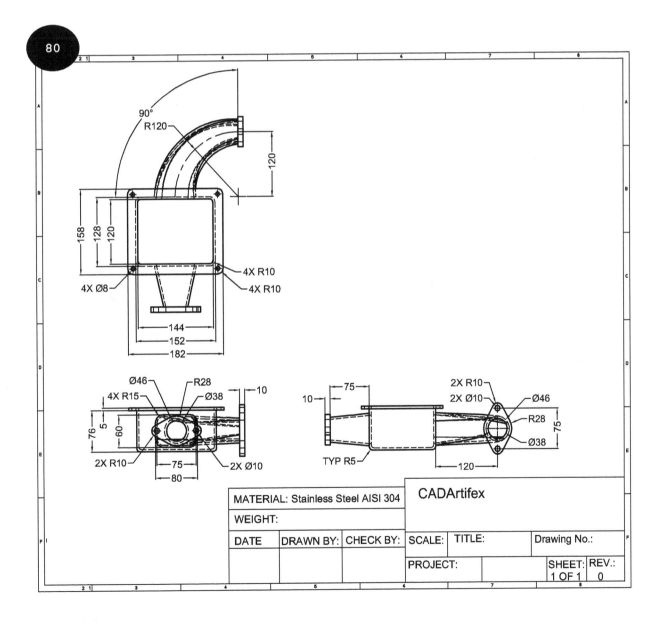

Exercise 41.

Create the 3D model, as shown in Figure 81. Different views of the model and dimensions are shown in Figure 82. After creating the model, assign the Steel AISI 1020 107 HR material and calculate its mass properties. All dimensions are in mm.

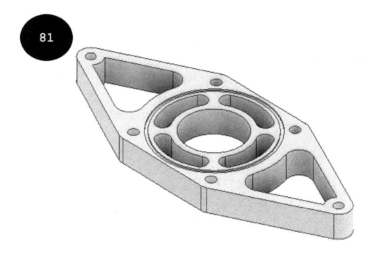

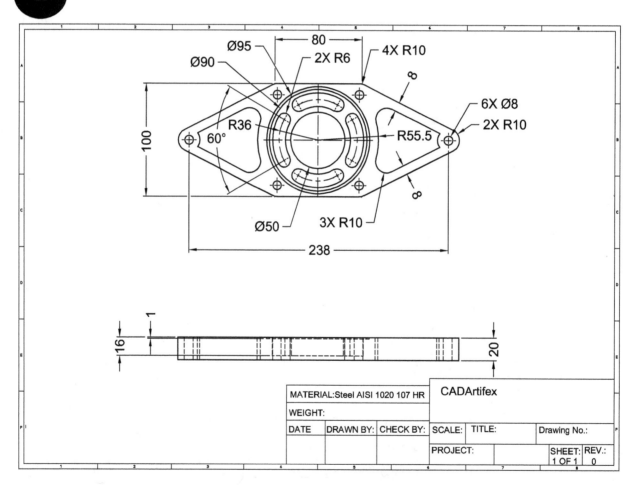

Exercise 42.

Create the 3D model, as shown in Figure 83. Different views of the model and dimensions are shown in Figure 84. After creating the model, assign the Steel, Alloy material and calculate its mass properties. All dimensions are in mm.

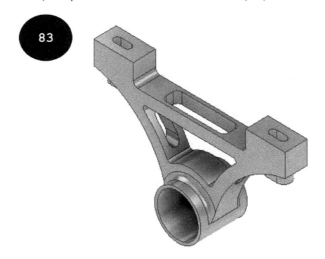

83

84

MATERIAL: Steel, Alloy

WEIGHT:

CADArtifex

DATE	DRAWN BY:	CHECK BY:	SCALE:	TITLE:		Drawing No.:	
			PROJECT:			SHEET: 1 OF 1	REV.: 0

Exercise 43.

Create the 3D model, as shown in Figure 85. Different views of the model and dimensions are shown in Figure 86. After creating the model, assign the Steel, Carbon material and calculate its mass properties. All dimensions are in mm.

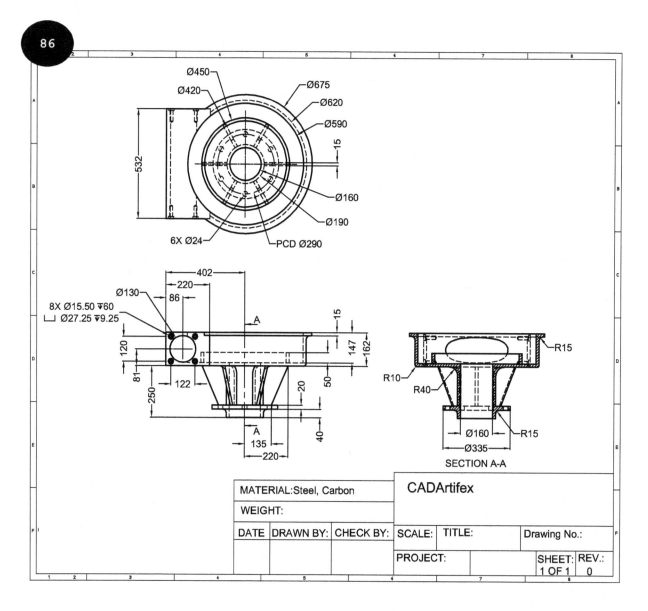

Exercise 44.

Create the 3D model, as shown in Figure 87. Different views of the model and dimensions are shown in Figure 88. After creating the model, assign the Stainless Steel AISI 304 material and calculate its mass properties. All dimensions are in mm.

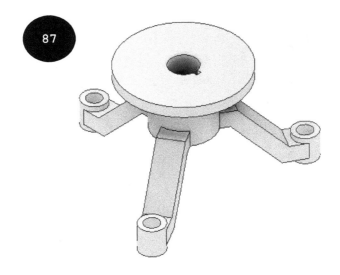

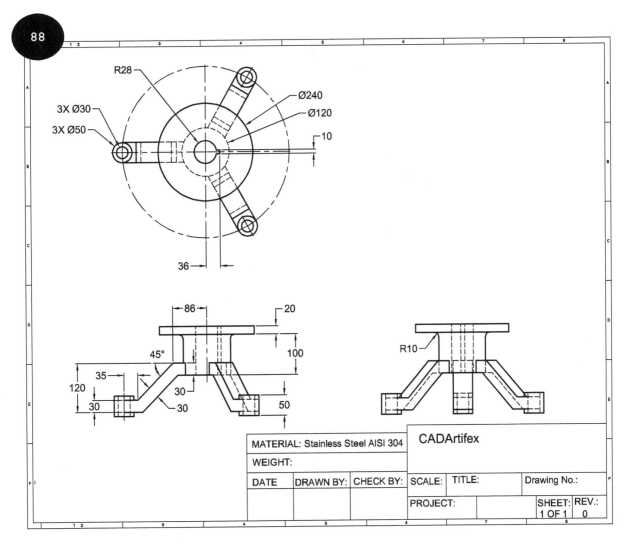

Exercise 45.

Create the 3D model, as shown in Figure 89. Different views of the model and dimensions are shown in Figure 90. After creating the model, assign the Steel AISI 1020 107 HR material and calculate its mass properties. All dimensions are in mm.

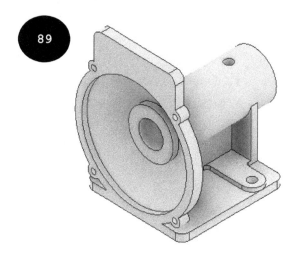

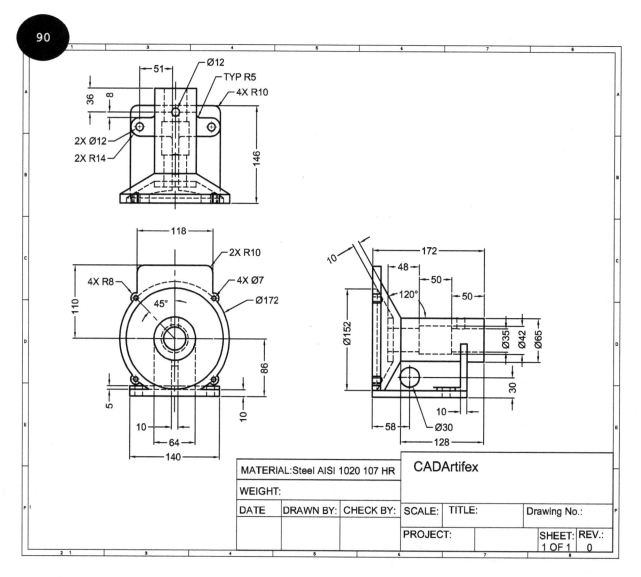

Exercise 46.

Create the 3D model, as shown in Figure 91. Different views of the model and dimensions are shown in Figure 92. After creating the model, assign the Steel, Alloy material and calculate its mass properties. All dimensions are in mm.

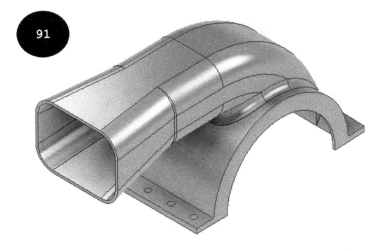

91

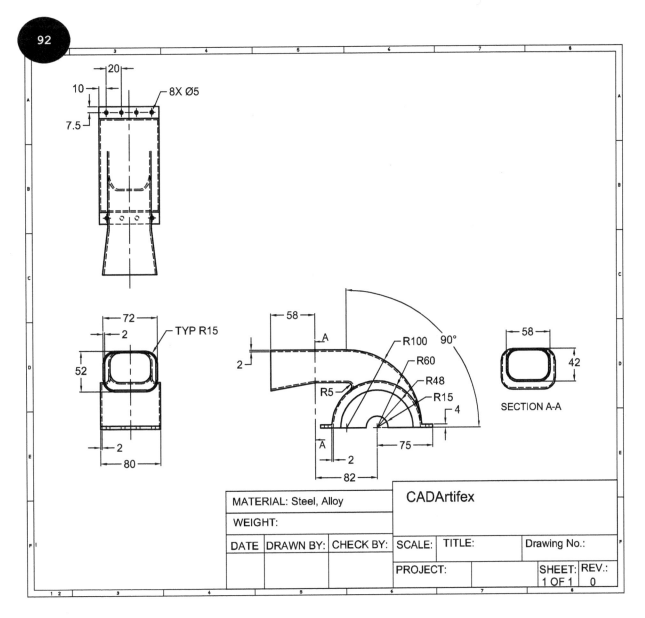

92

Exercise 47.

Create the 3D model, as shown in Figure 93. Different views of the model and dimensions are shown in Figure 94. After creating the model, assign the Steel, Carbon material and calculate its mass properties. All dimensions are in mm.

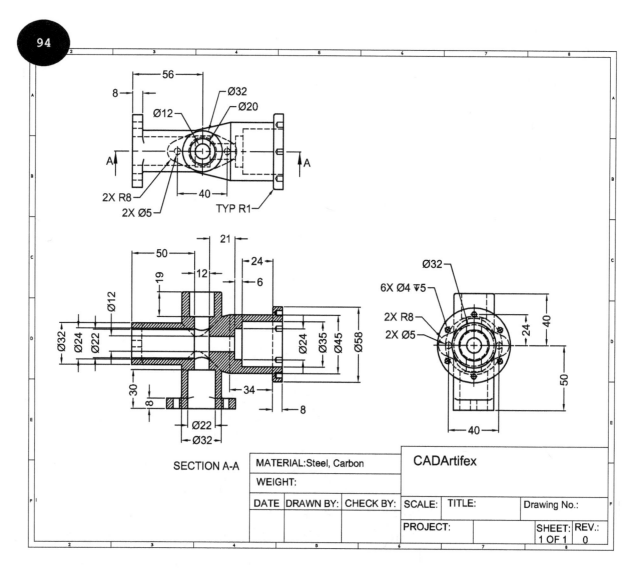

Exercise 48.

Create the 3D model, as shown in Figure 95. Different views of the model and dimensions are shown in Figure 96. After creating the model, assign the Stainless Steel AISI 304 material and calculate its mass properties. All dimensions are in mm.

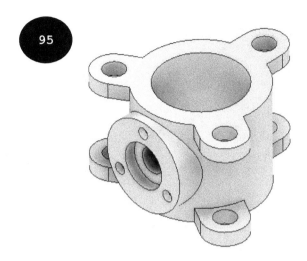

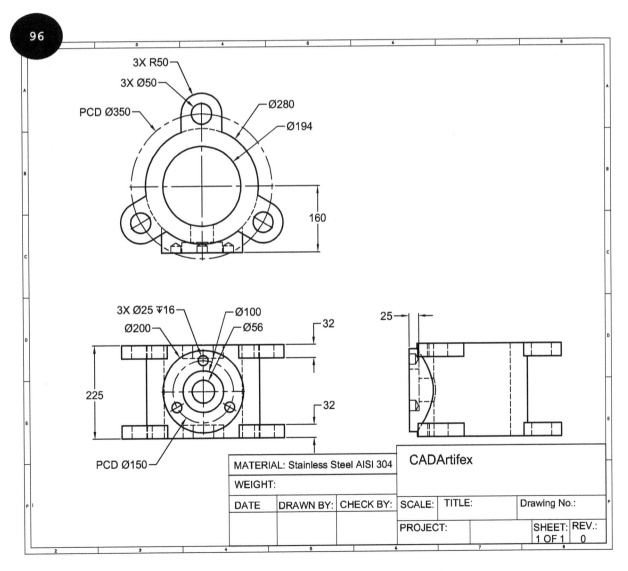

Exercise 49.

Create the 3D model, as shown in Figure 97. Different views of the model and dimensions are shown in Figure 98. After creating the model, assign the Steel AISI 1020 107 HR material and calculate its mass properties. All dimensions are in mm.

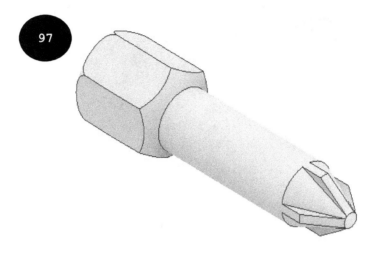

97

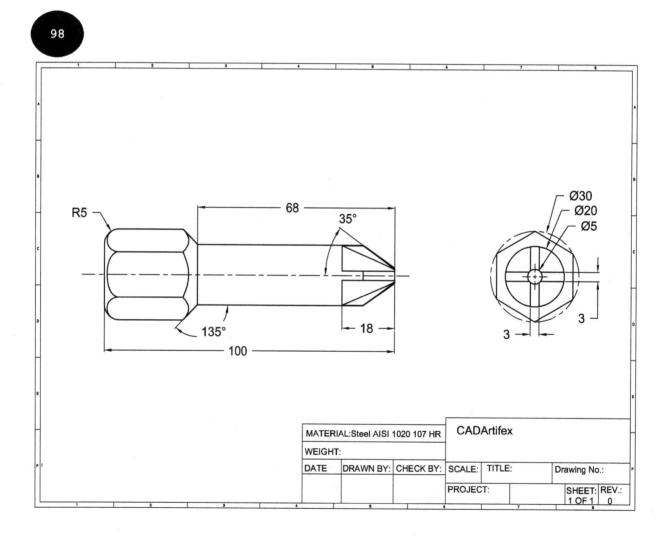

98

Exercise 50.

Create the 3D model, as shown in Figure 99. Different views of the model and dimensions are shown in Figure 100. After creating the model, assign the Steel, Alloy material and calculate its mass properties. All dimensions are in mm.

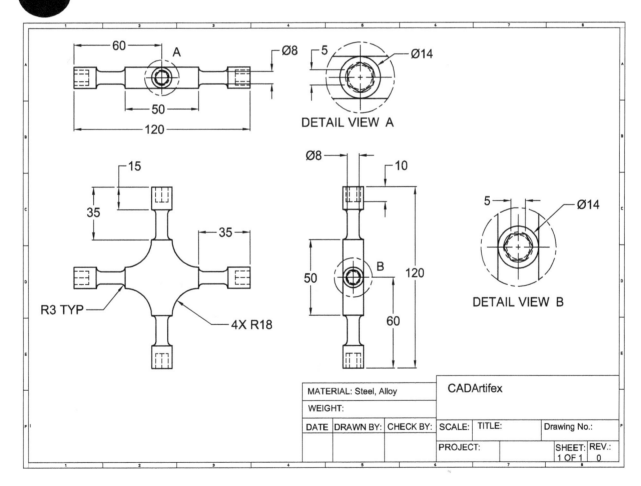

Exercise 51.

Create the 3D model, as shown in Figure 101. Different views of the model and dimensions are shown in Figure 102. After creating the model, assign the Steel, Alloy material and calculate its mass properties. All dimensions are in mm.

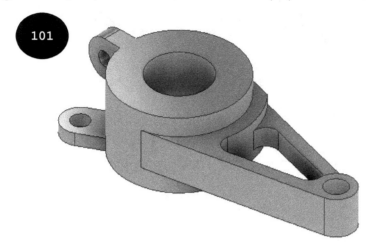

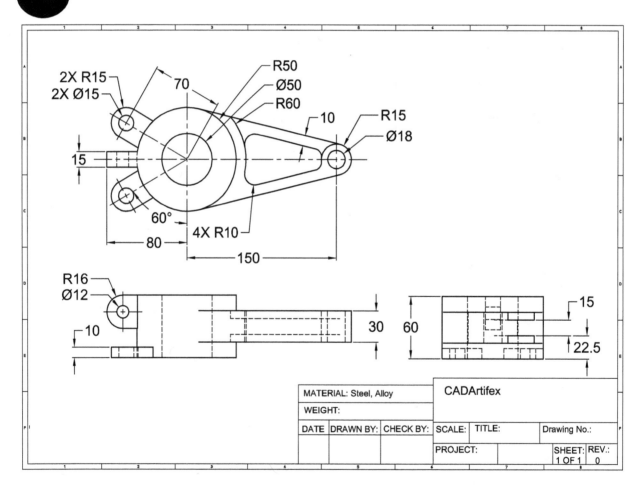

Exercise 52.

Create the 3D model, as shown in Figure 103. Different views and dimensions are shown in Figure 104. After creating the model, assign the Steel, Carbon material and calculate its mass properties. All dimensions are in mm.

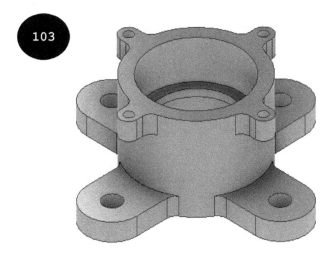

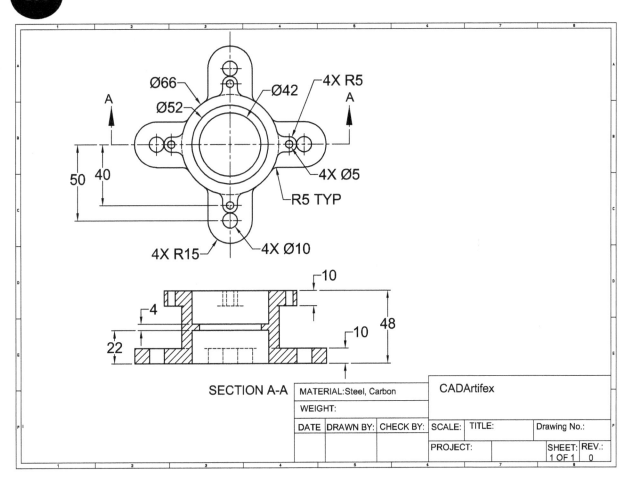

Exercise 53.

Create the 3D model, as shown in Figure 105. Different views of the model and dimensions are shown in Figure 106. After creating the model, assign the Steel, Carbon material and calculate its mass properties. All dimensions are in mm.

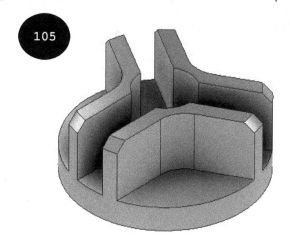

105

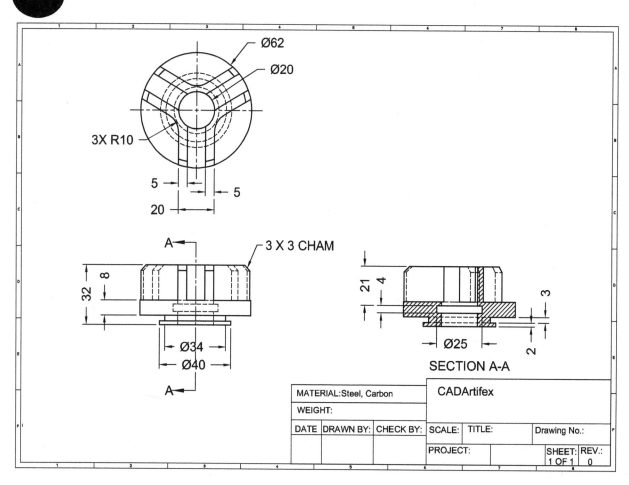

106

Exercise 54.

Create the 3D model, as shown in Figure 107. Different views of the model and dimensions are shown in Figure 108. After creating the model, assign the Stainless Steel AISI 304 material and calculate its mass properties. All dimensions are in mm.

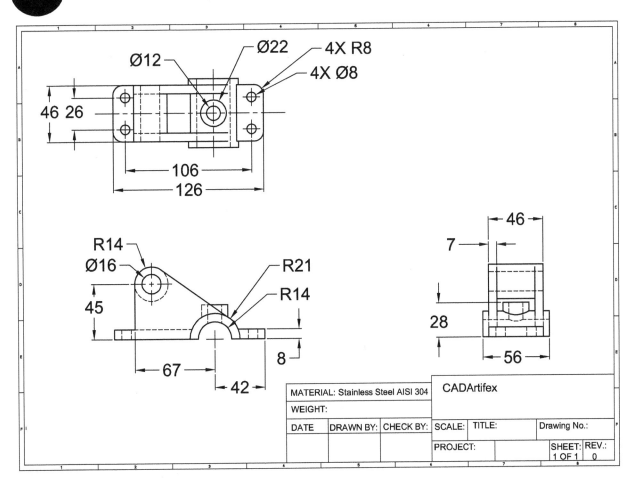

Exercise 55.

Create the 3D model, as shown in Figure 109. Different views of the model and dimensions are shown in Figure 110. After creating the model, assign the Stainless Steel AISI 304 material and calculate its mass properties. All dimensions are in mm.

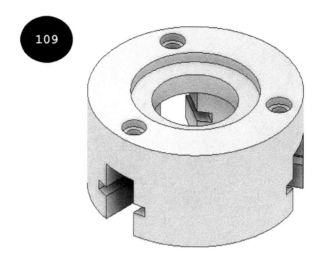

109

110

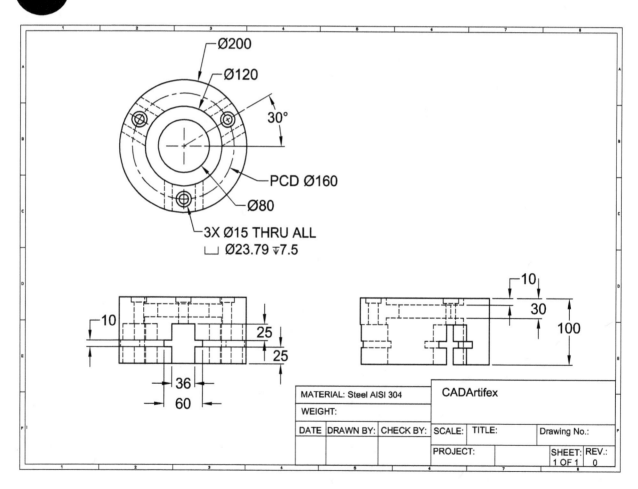

Exercise 56.

Create the 3D model, as shown in Figure 111. Different views of the model and dimensions are shown in Figure 112. After creating the model, assign the Steel AISI 1020 107 HR material and calculate its mass properties. All dimensions are in mm.

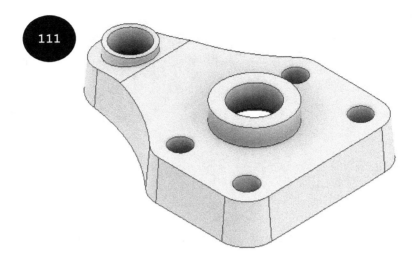

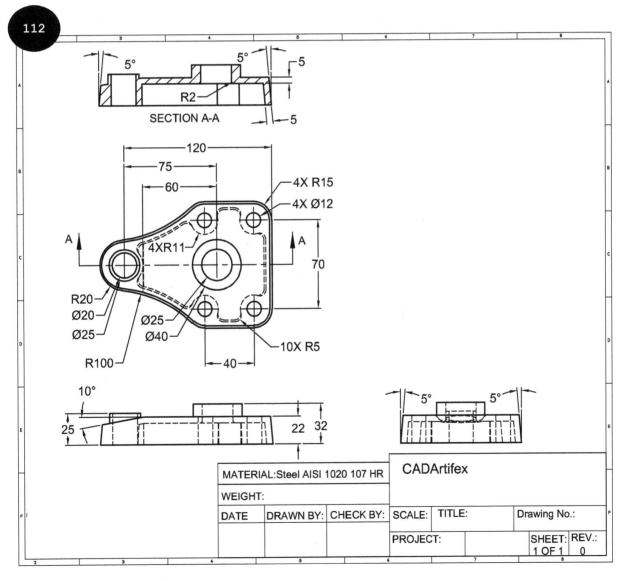

Exercise 57.

Create the 3D model, as shown in Figure 113. Different views and dimensions are shown in Figure 114. After creating the model, assign the Steel, Carbon material and calculate its mass properties. All dimensions are in mm.

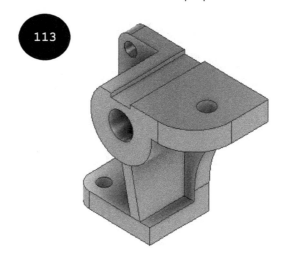

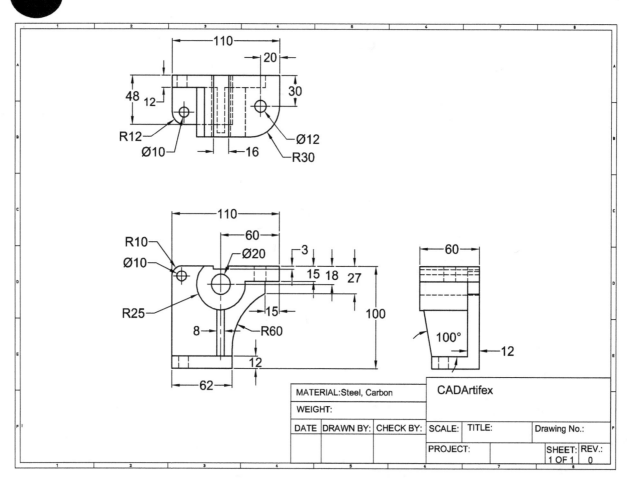

Exercise 58.

Create the 3D model, as shown in Figure 115. Different views of the model and dimensions are shown in Figure 116. After creating the model, assign the Steel, Alloy material and calculate its mass properties. All dimensions are in mm.

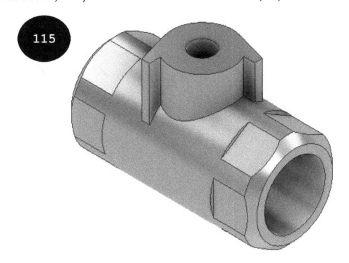

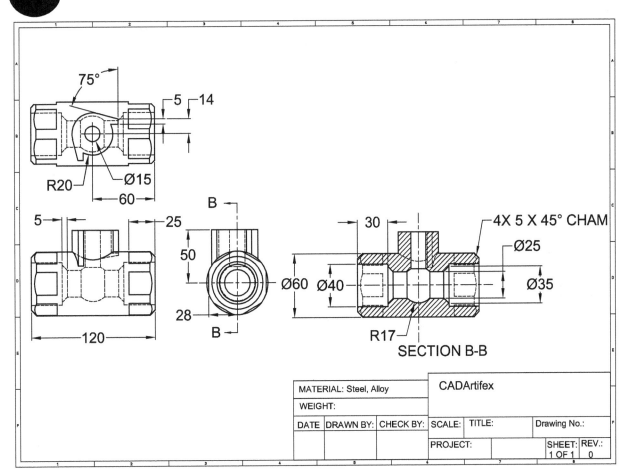

Exercise 59.

Create the 3D model, as shown in Figure 117. Different views of the model and dimensions are shown in Figure 118. After creating the model, assign the Steel, Carbon material and calculate its mass properties. All dimensions are in mm.

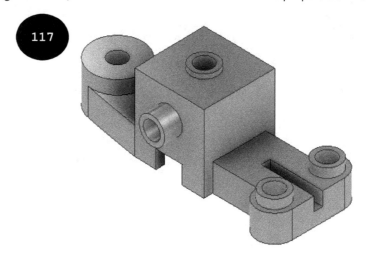

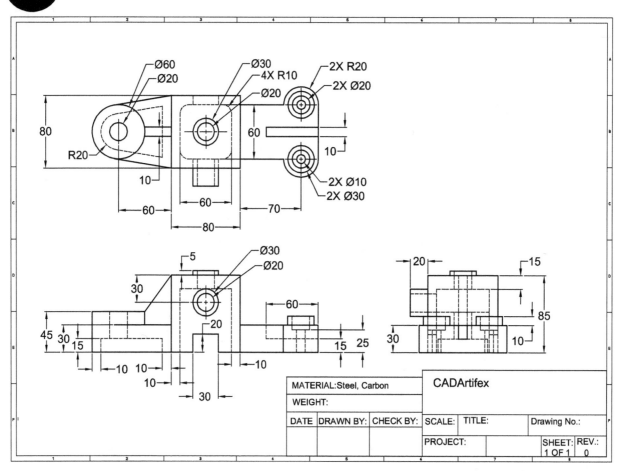

Exercise 60.

Create the 3D model, as shown in Figure 119. Different views of the model and dimensions are shown in Figure 120. After creating the model, assign the Stainless Steel AISI 304 material and calculate its mass properties. All dimensions are in mm.

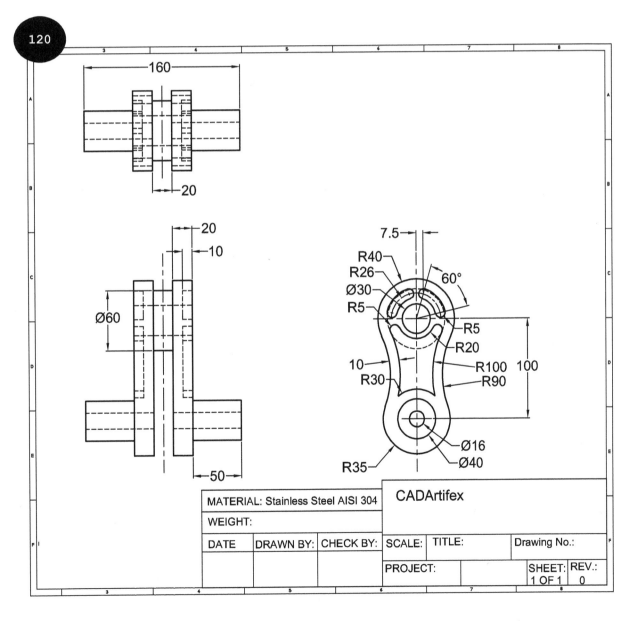

Exercise 61.

Create the 3D model, as shown in Figure 121. Different views of the model and dimensions are shown in Figure 122. After creating the model, assign the Stainless Steel AISI 304 material and calculate its mass properties. All dimensions are in mm.

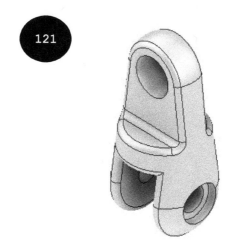

121

122

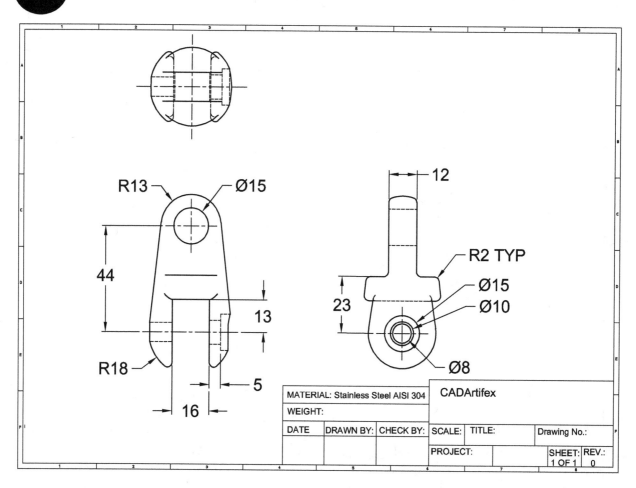

R13 Ø15

44

13

R18

5

16

12

R2 TYP

Ø15

Ø10

23

Ø8

MATERIAL: Stainless Steel AISI 304		CADArtifex		
WEIGHT:				
DATE	DRAWN BY: CHECK BY:	SCALE: TITLE:		Drawing No.:
		PROJECT:		SHEET: REV.: 1 OF 1 0

Exercise 62.

Create the 3D model, as shown in Figure 123. Different views of the model and dimensions are shown in Figure 124. After creating the model, assign the Steel, Carbon material and calculate its mass properties. All dimensions are in mm.

123

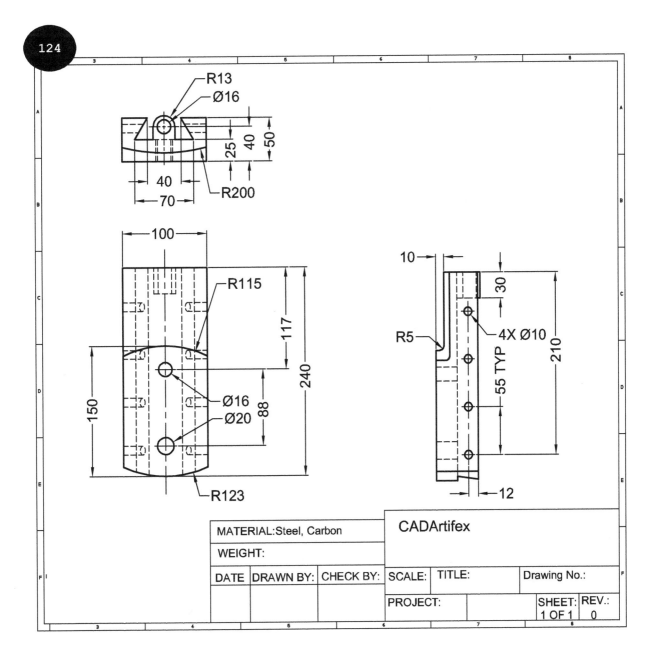

124

Exercise 63.

Create the 3D model, as shown in Figure 125. Different views of the model and dimensions are shown in Figure 126. After creating the model, assign the Steel AISI 1020 107 HR material and calculate its mass properties. All dimensions are in mm.

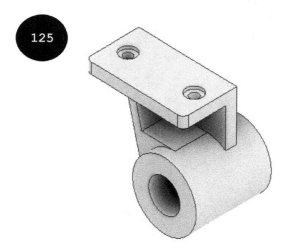

125

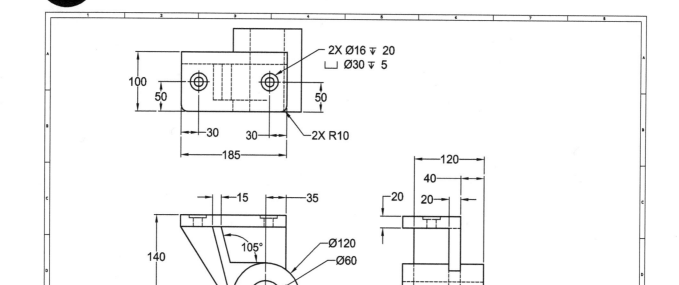

126

Exercise 64.

Create the 3D model, as shown in Figure 127. Different views of the model and dimensions are shown in Figure 128. After creating the model, assign the Steel, Alloy material and calculate its mass properties. All dimensions are in mm.

127

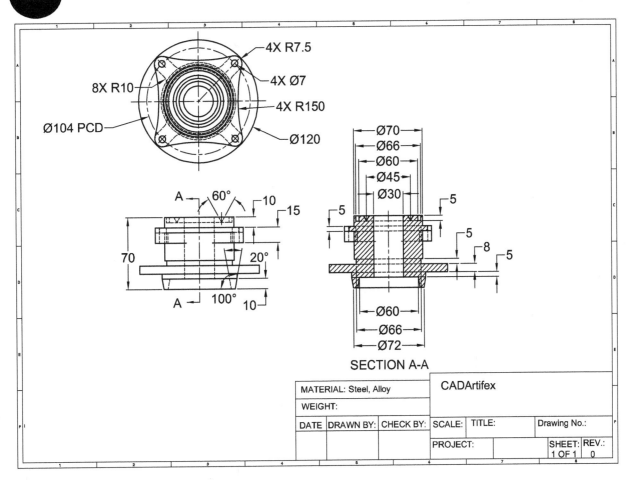

128

4X R7.5

4X Ø7

8X R10

4X R150

Ø104 PCD

Ø120

Ø70
Ø66
Ø60
Ø45
Ø30

A
60°
10
15
5
5
5
8
5
70
20°
Ø60
Ø66
Ø72
A
100°
10

SECTION A-A

MATERIAL: Steel, Alloy		CADArtifex		
WEIGHT:				
DATE	DRAWN BY:	CHECK BY:	SCALE:	TITLE:
			PROJECT:	

Drawing No.:

SHEET: REV.:
1 OF 1   0

Exercise 65.

Create the 3D model, as shown in Figure 129. Different views and dimensions are shown in Figure 130. After creating the model, assign the Steel, Carbon material and calculate its mass properties. All dimensions are in mm.

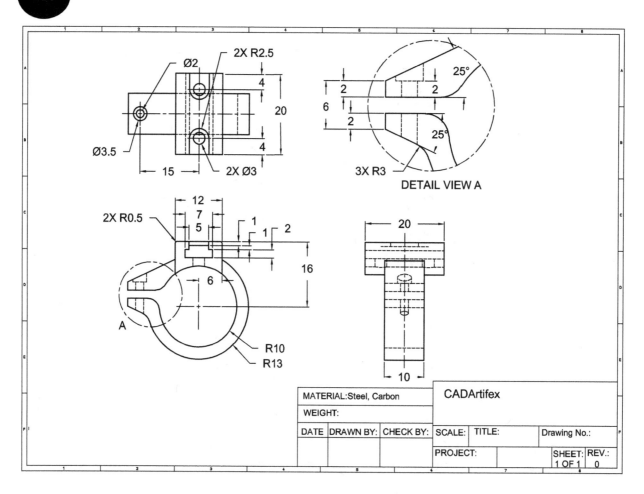

Exercise 66.

Create the 3D model, as shown in Figure 131. Different views of the model and dimensions are shown in Figure 132. After creating the model, assign the Steel, Alloy material and calculate its mass properties. All dimensions are in mm.

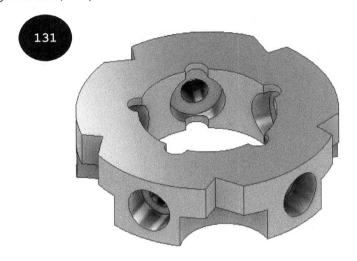

131

132

21

90°

12.5

Ø12

Ø6

Ø60 PCD

5X R10

36°

Ø10

56°

18

22

R15

R28.5

5X R2.5

SECTION A-A

A

7.5

15

A

MATERIAL: Steel, Alloy			CADArtifex		
WEIGHT:					
DATE	DRAWN BY:	CHECK BY:	SCALE:	TITLE:	Drawing No.:
			PROJECT:		SHEET: 1 OF 1 / REV.: 0

Exercise 67.

Create the 3D model, as shown in Figure 133. Different views of the model and dimensions are shown in Figure 134. After creating the model, assign the Stainless Steel AISI 304 material and calculate its mass properties. All dimensions are in mm.

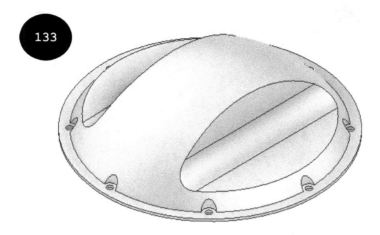

133

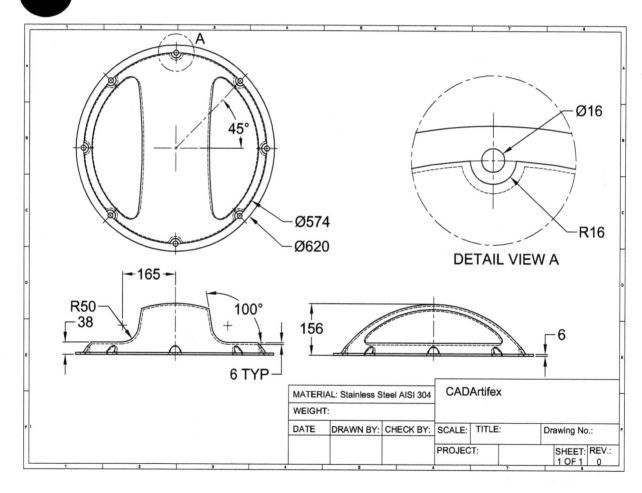

134

DETAIL VIEW A

Ø574
Ø620
Ø16
R16
45°
165
R50
38
100°
6 TYP
156
6

MATERIAL: Stainless Steel AISI 304		CADArtifex		
WEIGHT:				
DATE	DRAWN BY:	CHECK BY:	SCALE:	TITLE:	Drawing No.:
			PROJECT:		SHEET: 1 OF 1	REV.: 0

Exercise 68.

Create the 3D model, as shown in Figure 135. Different views of the model and dimensions are shown in Figure 136. After creating the model, assign the Steel AISI 1020 107 HR material and calculate its mass properties. All dimensions are in mm.

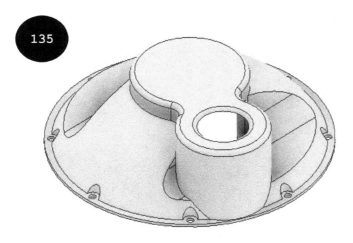

135

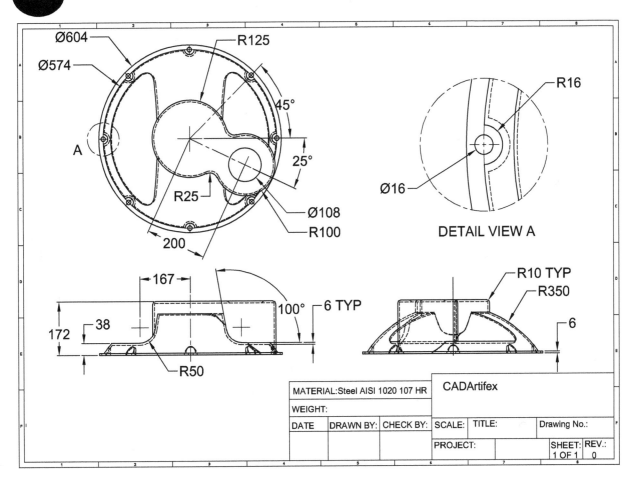

136

Exercise 69.

Create the 3D model, as shown in Figure 137. Different views of the model and dimensions are shown in Figure 138. After creating the model, assign the Stainless Steel AISI 304 material and calculate its mass properties. All dimensions are in mm.

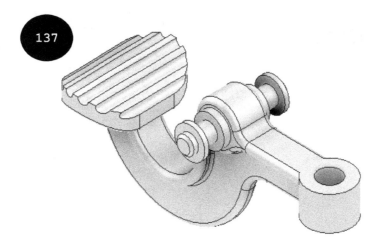

137

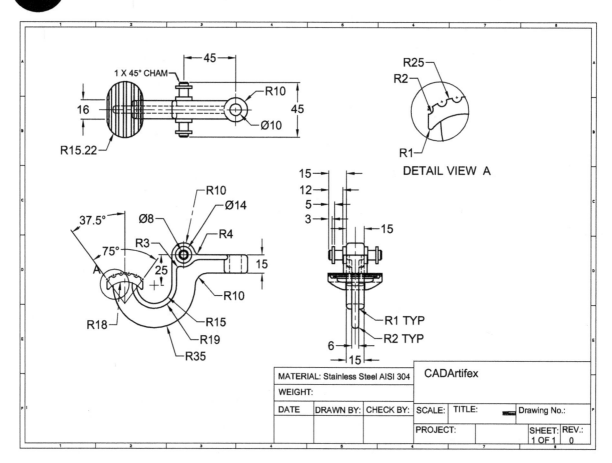

138

Exercise 70.

Create the 3D model, as shown in Figure 139. Different views of the model and dimensions are shown in Figure 140. After creating the model, assign the Steel, Carbon material and calculate its mass properties. All dimensions are in mm.

139

140

SECTION A-A
5
30
3X R12
C

DETAIL VIEW C
2
2
1
8

Ø100
A — A

SECTION B-B
B
B
40
70
2X R10

60 48
10
Ø30
Ø20
2X R8

MATERIAL:Steel, Carbon			CADArtifex			
WEIGHT:						
DATE	DRAWN BY:	CHECK BY:	SCALE:	TITLE:		Drawing No.:
			PROJECT:			SHEET: REV.:
						1 OF 1 0

Exercise 71.

Create the 3D model, as shown in Figure 141. Different views of the model and dimensions are shown in Figure 142. After creating the model, assign the Stainless Steel AISI 304 material and calculate its mass properties. All dimensions are in mm.

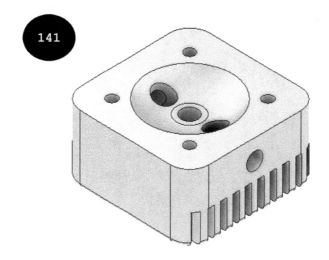

141

142

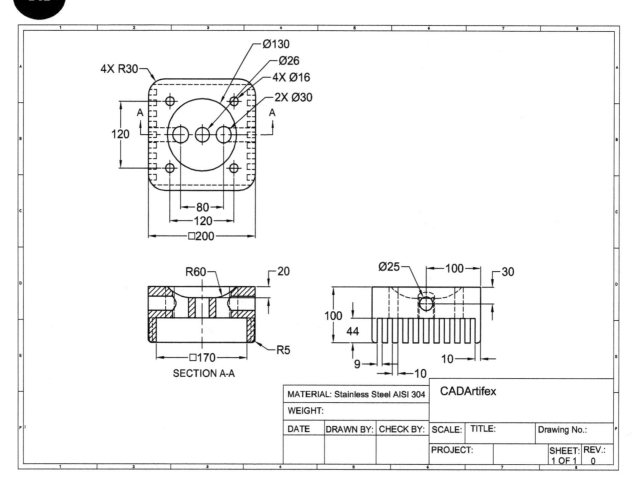

Exercise 72.

Create the 3D model, as shown in Figure 143. Different views of the model and dimensions are shown in Figure 144. After creating the model, assign the Stainless Steel AISI 304 material and calculate its mass properties. All dimensions are in mm.

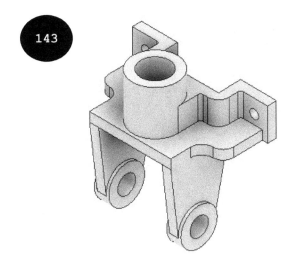

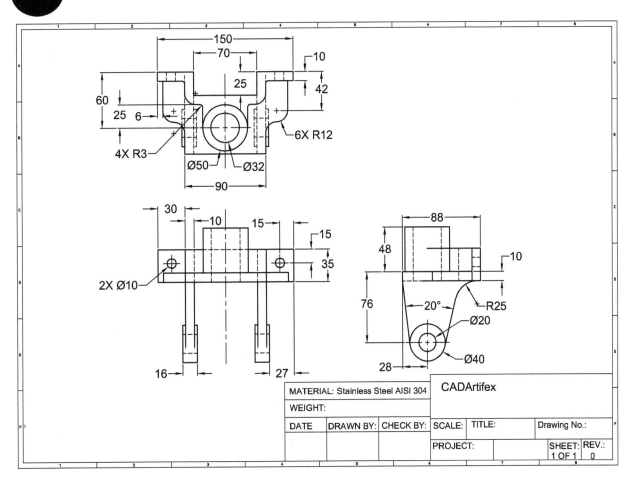

Exercise 73.

Create the 3D model, as shown in Figure 145. Different views of the model and dimensions are shown in Figure 146. After creating the model, assign the Steel AISI 1020 107 HR material and calculate its mass properties. All dimensions are in mm.

145

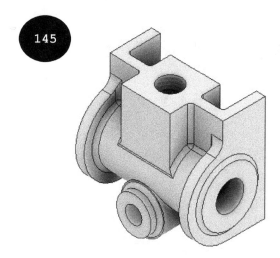

146

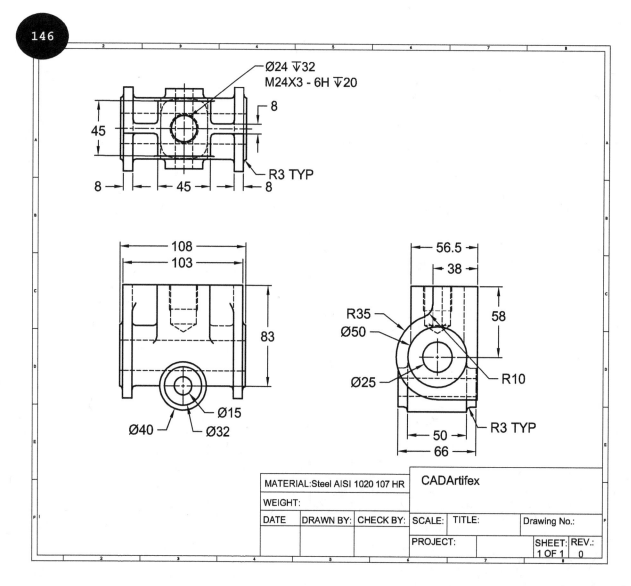

Ø24 ∇32
M24X3 - 6H ∇20

8

45

8 — 45 — 8

R3 TYP

108
103

83

Ø15
Ø40   Ø32

56.5
38

R35
Ø50

58

Ø25   R10

R3 TYP

50
66

MATERIAL:Steel AISI 1020 107 HR		CADArtifex		
WEIGHT:				
DATE	DRAWN BY:	CHECK BY:	SCALE:	TITLE:	Drawing No.:
			PROJECT:		SHEET: 1 OF 1	REV.: 0

Exercise 74.

Create the 3D model, as shown in Figure 147. Different views of the model and dimensions are shown in Figure 148. After creating the model, assign the Steel, Carbon material and calculate its mass properties. All dimensions are in mm.

147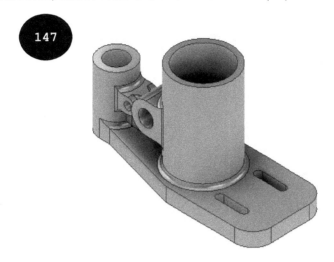

148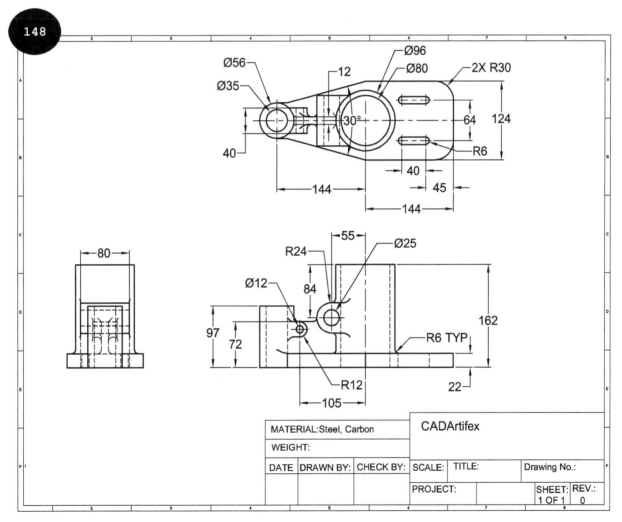

MATERIAL:Steel, Carbon			CADArtifex			
WEIGHT:						
DATE	DRAWN BY:	CHECK BY:	SCALE:	TITLE:		Drawing No.:
			PROJECT:			SHEET: 1 OF 1 / REV.: 0

Exercise 75.

Create the 3D model, as shown in Figure 149. Different views of the model and dimensions are shown in Figure 150. After creating the model, assign the Stainless Steel AISI 304 material and calculate its mass properties. All dimensions are in mm.

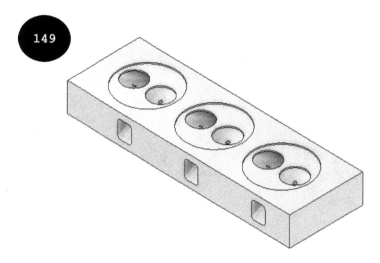

149

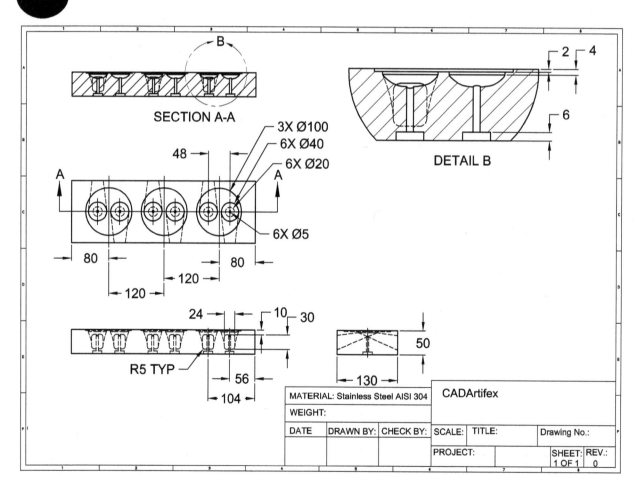

150

Exercise 76.

Create the 3D model, as shown in Figure 151. Different views of the model and dimensions are shown in Figure 152. After creating the model, assign the Steel, Carbon material and calculate its mass properties. All dimensions are in mm.

151

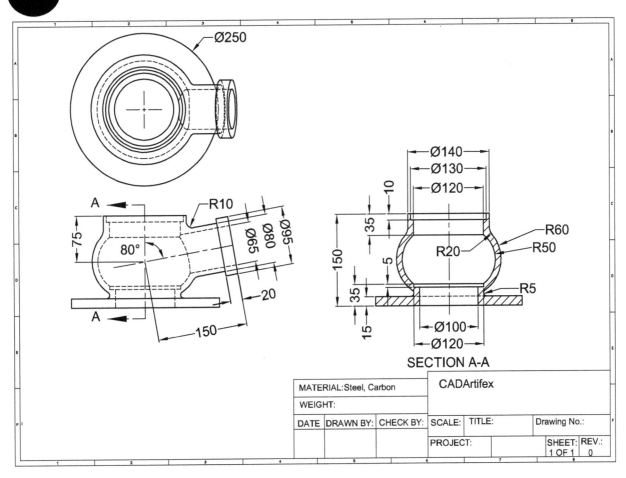

152

98

Exercise 77.

Create the 3D model, as shown in Figure 153. Different views of the model and dimensions are shown in Figure 154. After creating the model, assign the Stainless Steel AISI 304 material and calculate its mass properties. All dimensions are in mm.

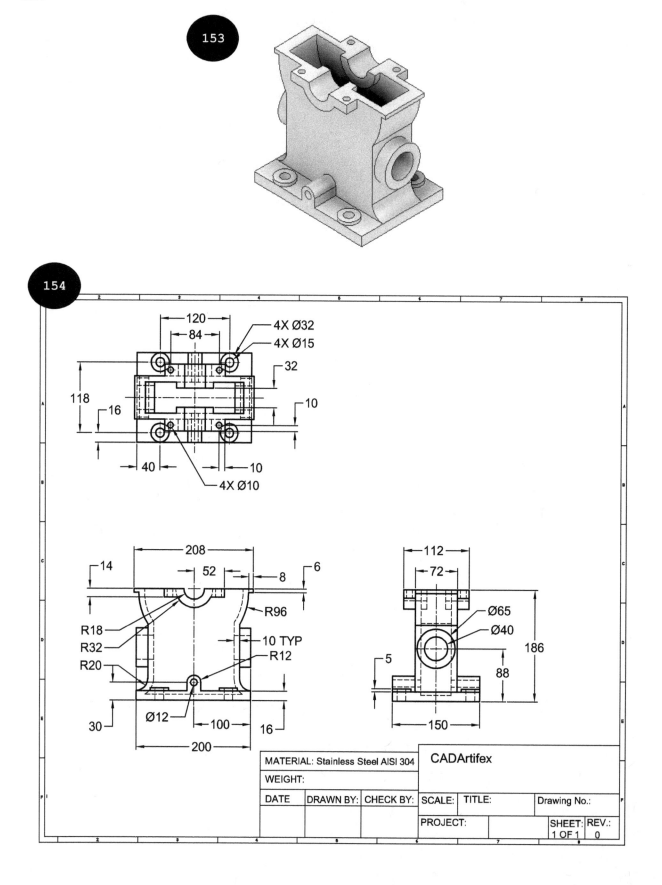

Exercise 78.

Create the 3D model, as shown in Figure 155. Different views of the model and dimensions are shown in Figure 156. After creating the model, assign the Steel AISI 1020 107 HR material and calculate its mass properties. All dimensions are in mm.

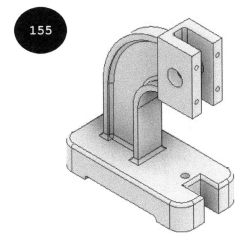

155

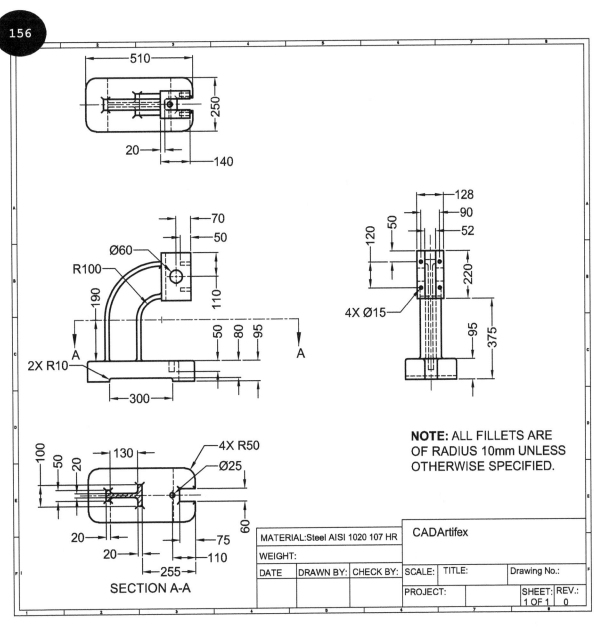

156

NOTE: ALL FILLETS ARE OF RADIUS 10mm UNLESS OTHERWISE SPECIFIED.

SECTION A-A

MATERIAL:Steel AISI 1020 107 HR			CADArtifex		
WEIGHT:					
DATE	DRAWN BY:	CHECK BY:	SCALE:	TITLE:	Drawing No.:
			PROJECT:		SHEET: 1 OF 1 / REV.: 0

Exercise 79.

Create the 3D model, as shown in Figure 157. Different views of the model and dimensions are shown in Figure 158. After creating the model, assign the Steel, Alloy material and calculate its mass properties. All dimensions are in mm.

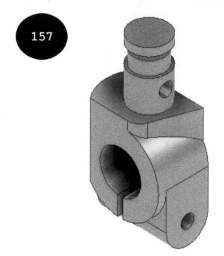

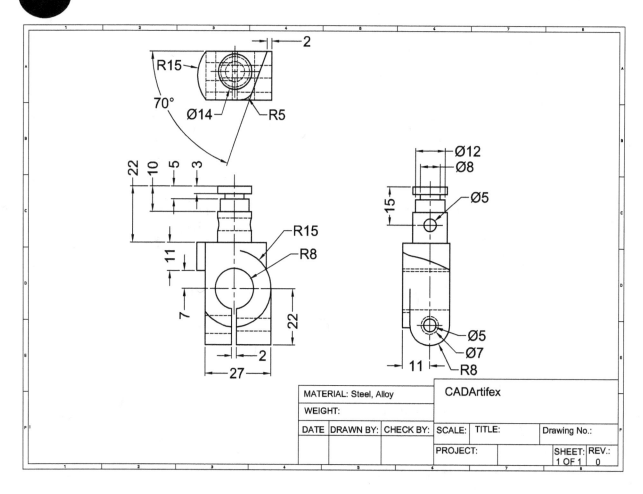

Exercise 80.

Create the 3D model, as shown in Figure 159. Different views of the model and dimensions are shown in Figure 160. After creating the model, assign the Steel, Carbon material and calculate its mass properties. All dimensions are in mm.

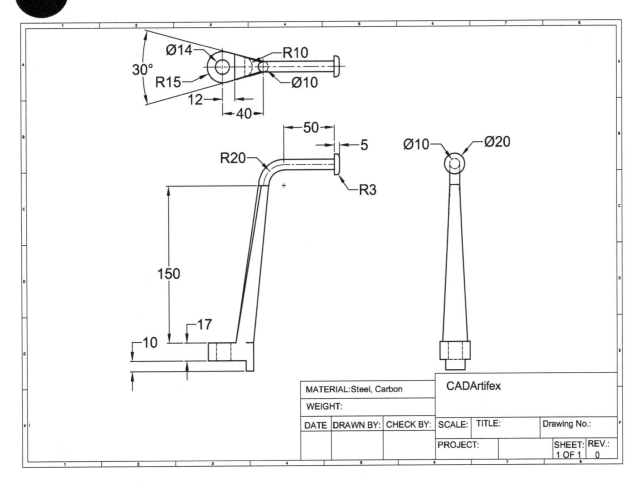

Exercise 81.

Create the 3D model, as shown in Figure 161. Different views of the model and dimensions are shown in Figure 162. After creating the model, assign the Stainless Steel AISI 304 material and calculate its mass properties. All dimensions are in mm.

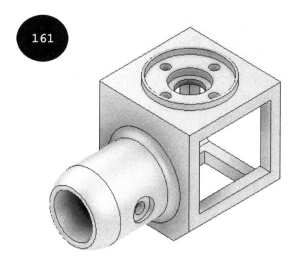

161

162

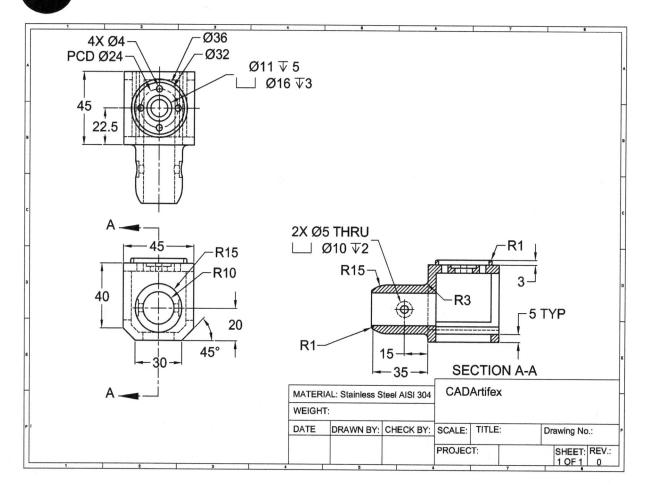

4X Ø4
PCD Ø24
Ø36
Ø32
Ø11 ⩖ 5
Ø16 ⩖ 3

45
22.5

A

45
R15
R10
40
20
30
45°

A

2X Ø5 THRU
Ø10 ⩖ 2
R15
R1
R3
R1
3
5 TYP
15
35

SECTION A-A

MATERIAL: Stainless Steel AISI 304		CADArtifex	
WEIGHT:			
DATE	DRAWN BY: CHECK BY:	SCALE: TITLE:	Drawing No.:
		PROJECT:	SHEET: 1 OF 1 REV.: 0

Exercise 82.

Create the 3D model, as shown in Figure 163. Different views of the model and dimensions are shown in Figure 164. After creating the model, assign the Steel, Alloy material and calculate its mass properties. All dimensions are in mm.

163

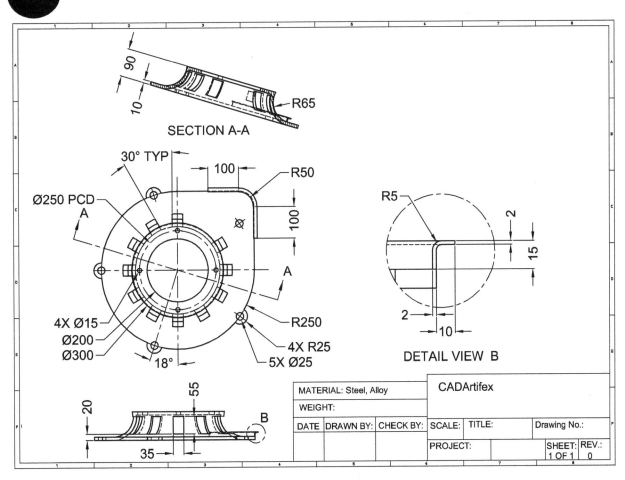

164

Exercise 83.

Create the 3D model, as shown in Figure 165. Different views of the model and dimensions are shown in Figure 166. After creating the model, assign the Steel AISI 1020 107 HR material and calculate its mass properties. All dimensions are in mm.

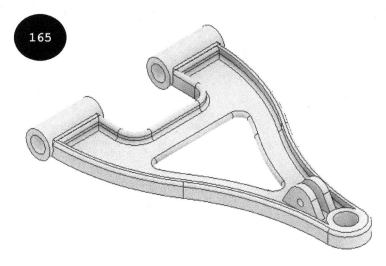

165

166

SECTION A-A

DETAIL VIEW B

MATERIAL:Steel AISI 1020 107 HR			CADArtifex		
WEIGHT:					
DATE	DRAWN BY:	CHECK BY:	SCALE:	TITLE:	Drawing No.:
			PROJECT:		SHEET: REV.: 1 OF 1 0

Exercise 84.

Create the 3D model, as shown in Figure 167. Different views of the model and dimensions are shown in Figure 168. After creating the model, assign the Steel, Alloy material and calculate its mass properties. All dimensions are in mm.

167

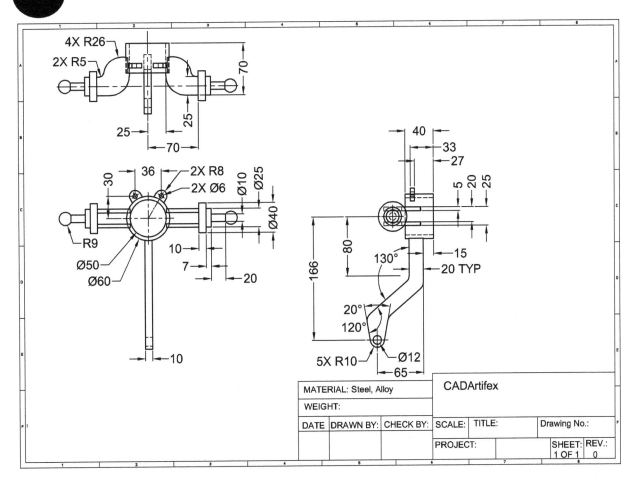

168

Exercise 85.

Create the 3D model, as shown in Figure 169. Different views of the model and dimensions are shown in Figure 170. After creating the model, assign the Stainless Steel AISI 304 material and calculate its mass properties. All dimensions are in mm.

169

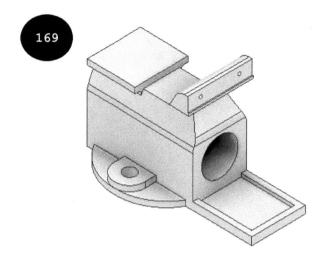

170

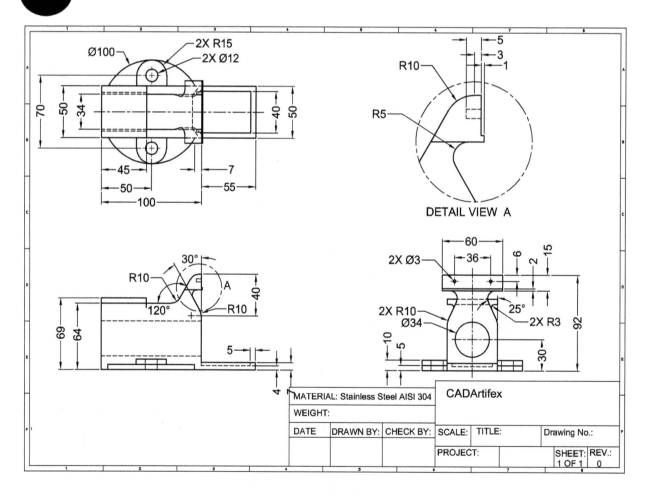

Exercise 86.

Create the 3D model, as shown in Figure 171. After creating the model, assign the Steel AISI 1020 107 HR material and calculate its mass properties. All dimensions are in mm.

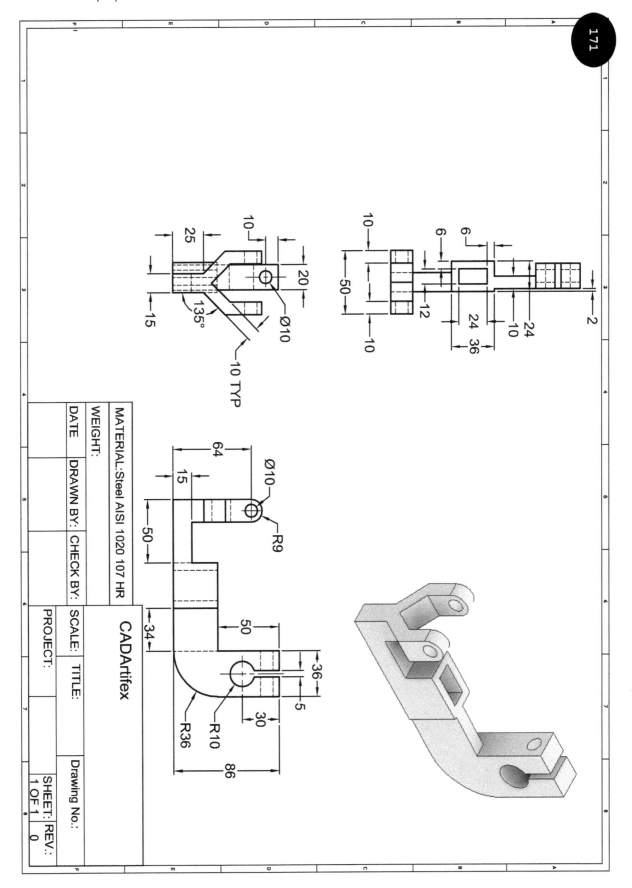

Exercise 87.

Create the 3D model, as shown in Figure 172. After creating the model, assign the Steel AISI 1020 107 HR material and calculate its mass properties. All dimensions are in mm.

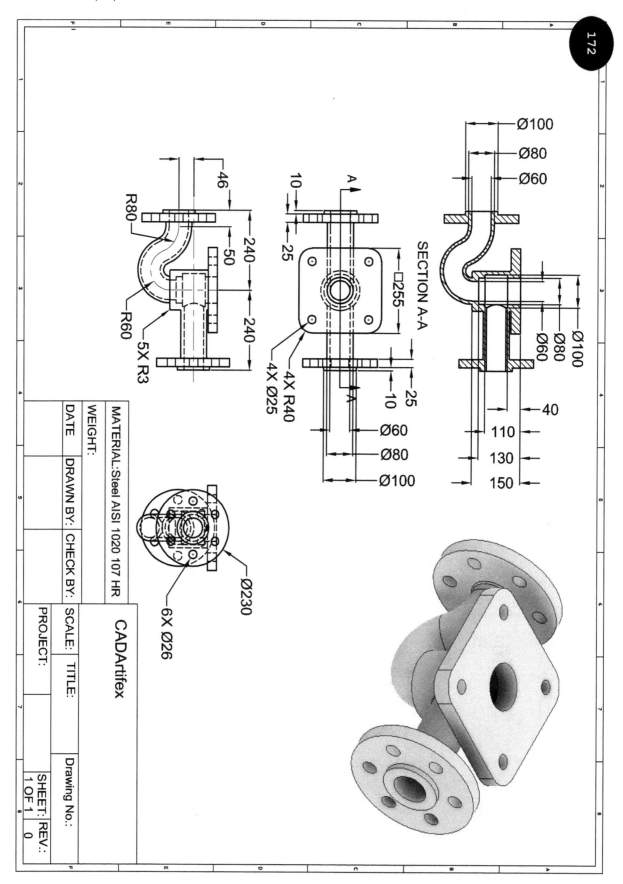

Exercise 88.

Create the 3D model, as shown in Figure 173. After creating the model, assign the Stainless Steel AISI 304 material and calculate its mass properties. All dimensions are in mm.

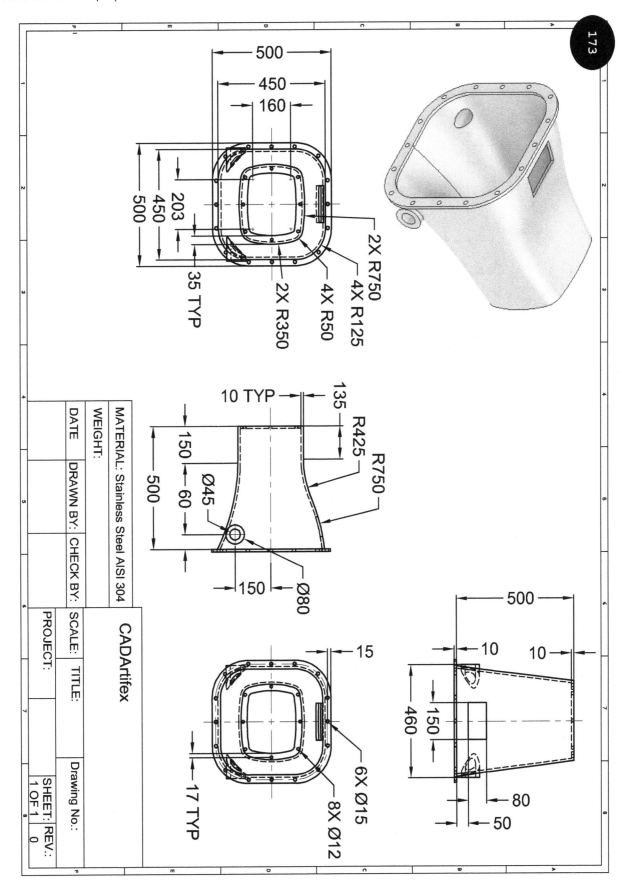

Exercise 89.

Create the 3D model, as shown in Figure 174. After creating the model, assign the Steel AISI 1020 107 HR material and calculate its mass properties. All dimensions are in mm.

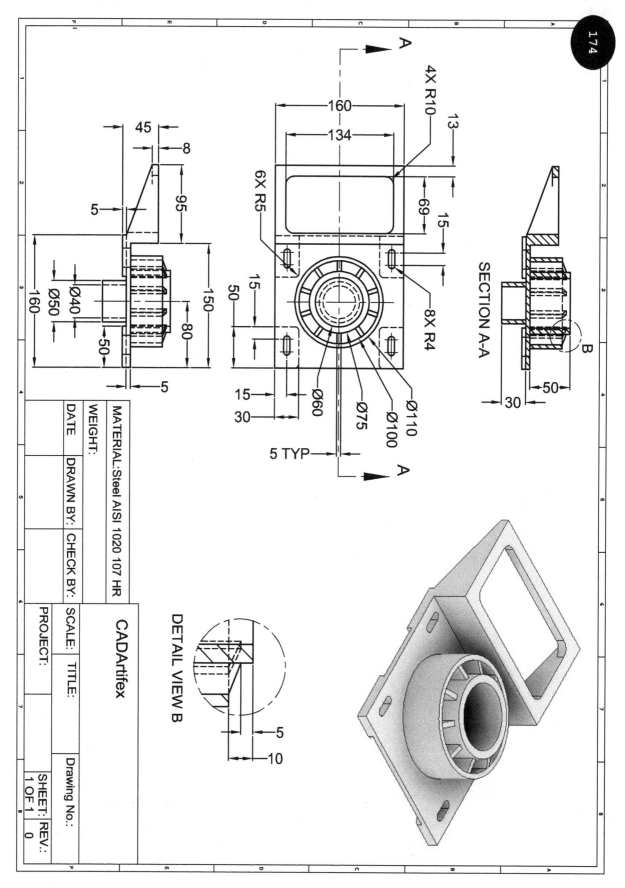

Exercise 90.

Create the 3D model, as shown in Figure 175. After creating the model, assign the Steel AISI 1020 107 HR material and calculate its mass properties. All dimensions are in mm.

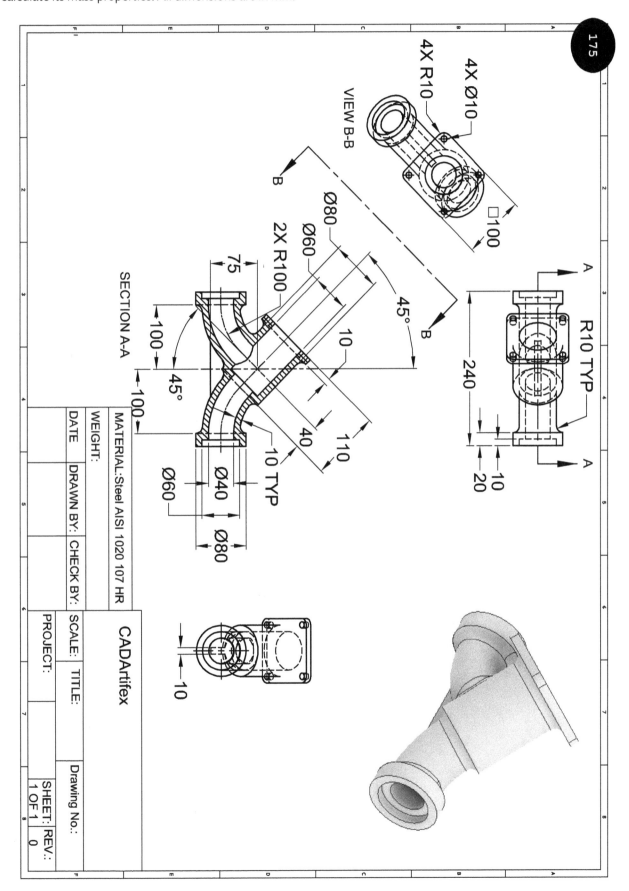

Exercise 91.

Create the 3D model, as shown in Figure 176. After creating the model, assign the Steel, Carbon material and calculate its mass properties. All dimensions are in mm.

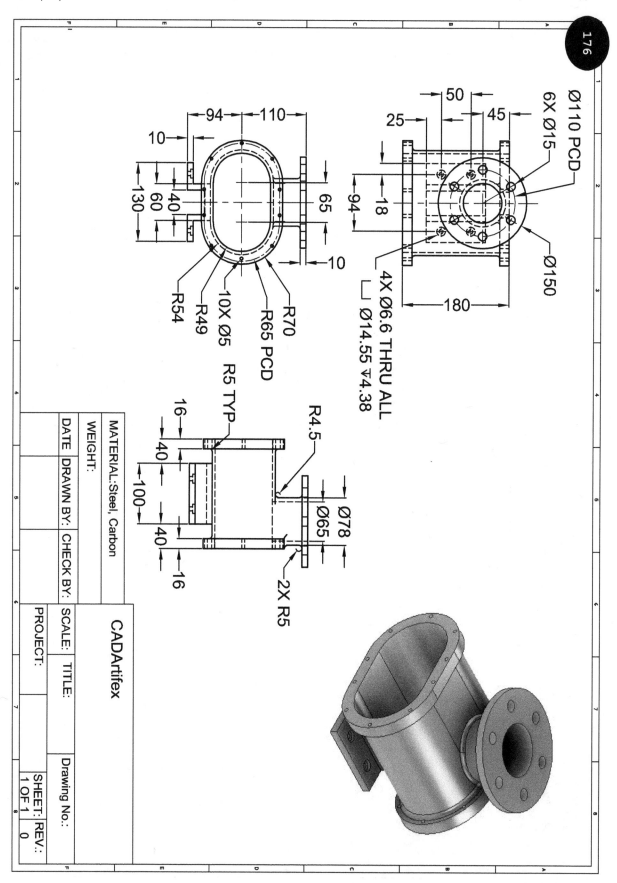

Exercise 92.

Create the 3D model, as shown in Figure 177. After creating the model, assign the Steel AISI 1020 107 HR material and calculate its mass properties. All dimensions are in mm.

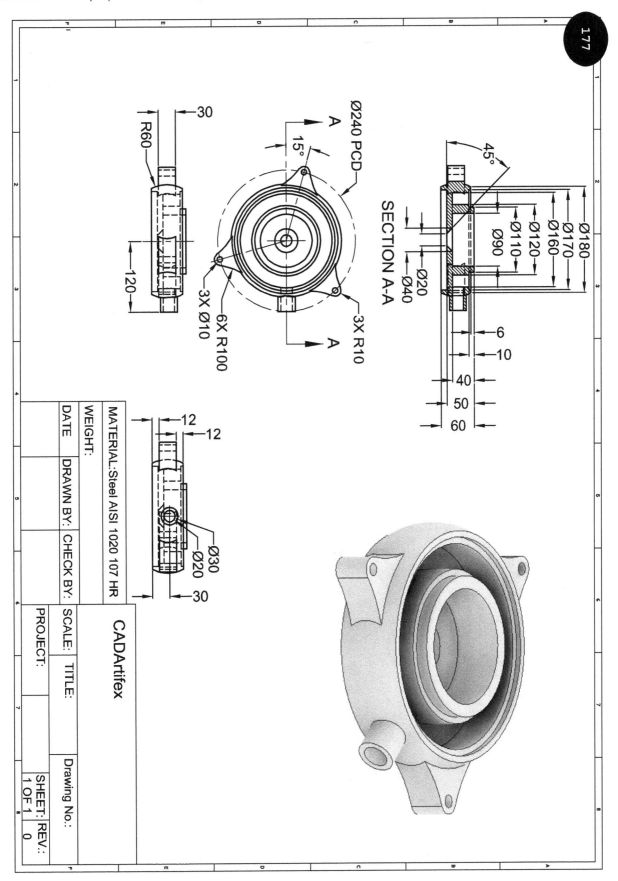

Exercise 93.

Create the 3D model, as shown in Figure 178. After creating the model, assign the Steel, Carbon material and calculate its mass properties. All dimensions are in mm.

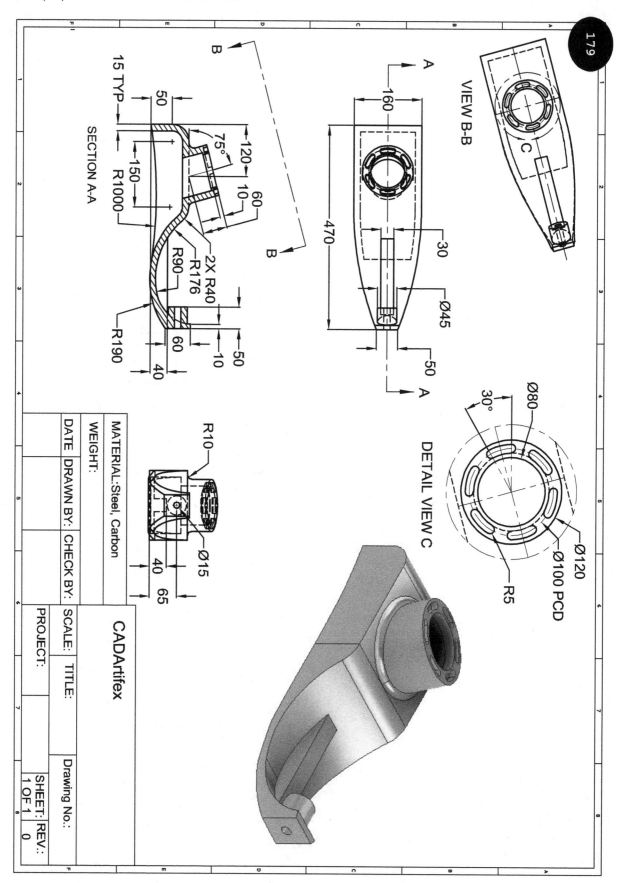

Exercise 94.

Create the 3D model, as shown in Figure 180. After creating the model, assign the Steel, Alloy material and calculate its mass properties. All dimensions are in mm.

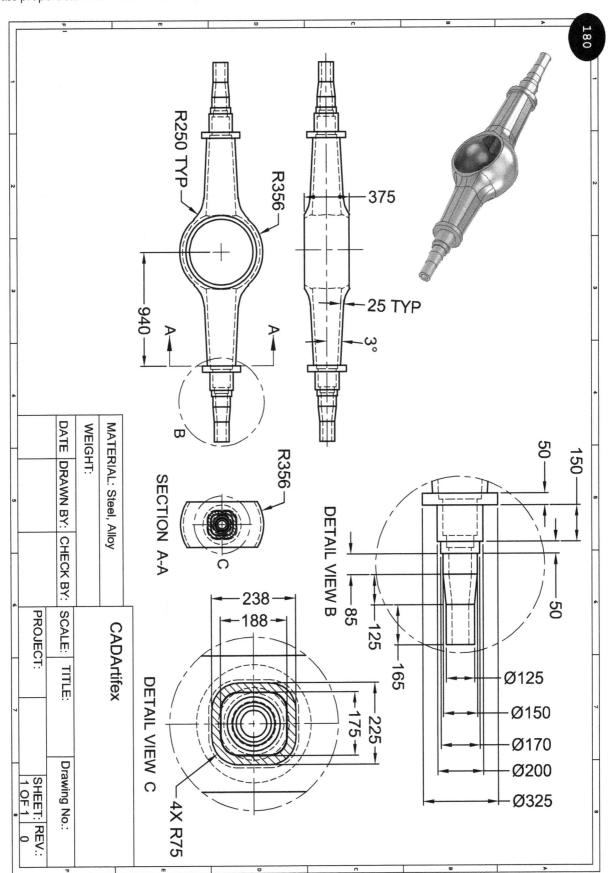

Exercise 95.

Create the 3D model, as shown in Figure 181. After creating the model, assign the Steel, Carbon material and calculate its mass properties. All dimensions are in mm.

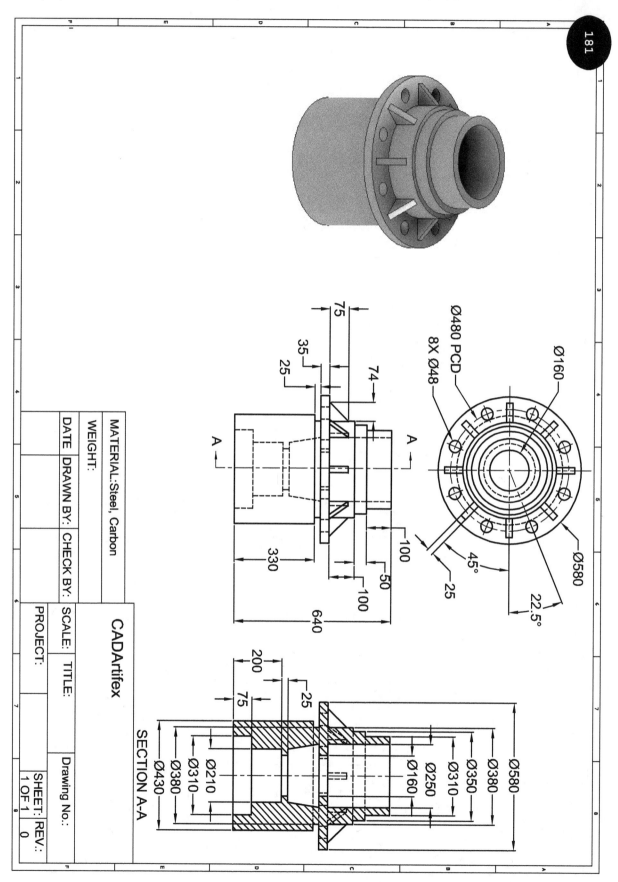

Exercise 96.

Create the 3D model, as shown in Figure 182. After creating the model, assign the Steel, Carbon material and calculate its mass properties. All dimensions are in mm.

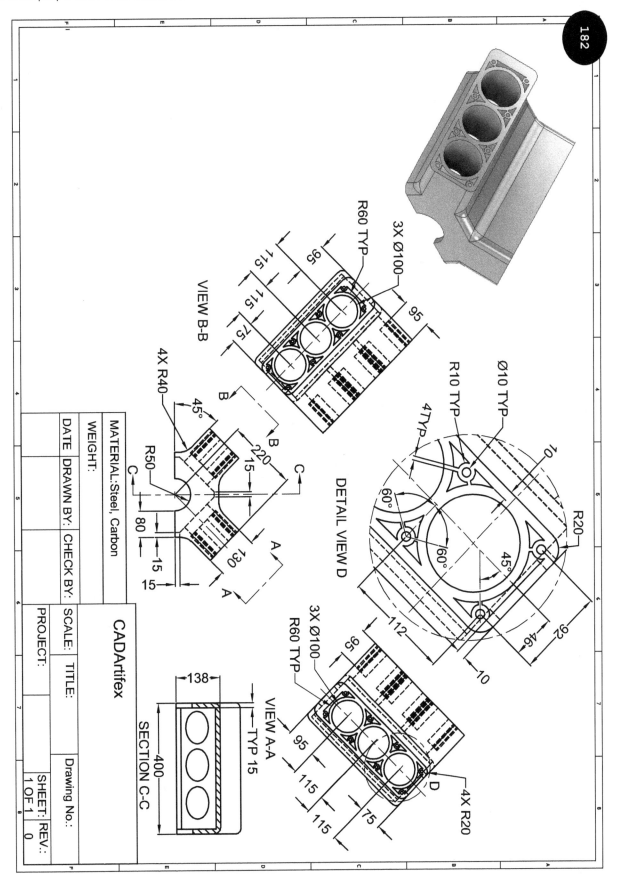

Exercise 97.

Create the 3D model, as shown in Figure 183. After creating the model, assign the Steel, Carbon material and calculate its mass properties. All dimensions are in mm.

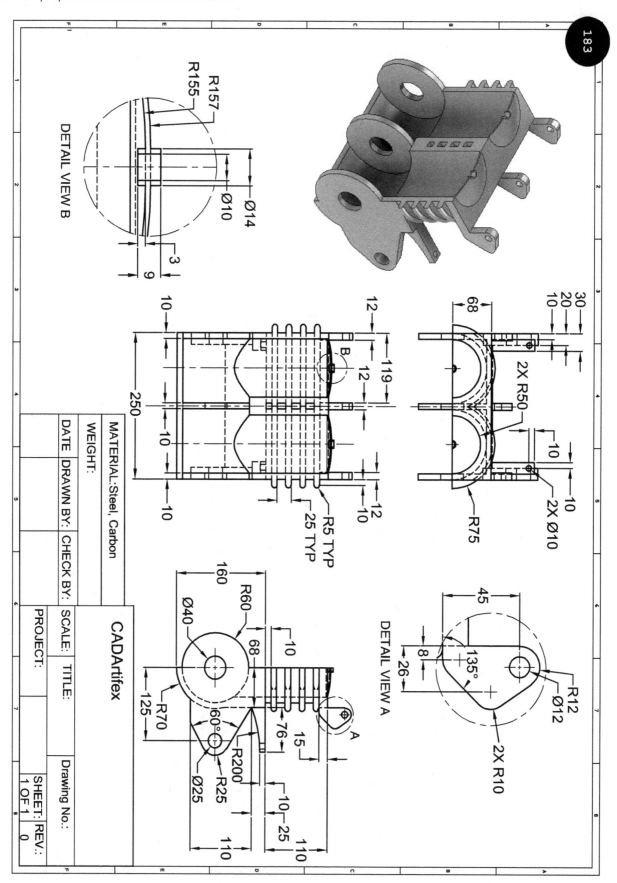

Exercise 98.

Create the 3D model, as shown in Figure 184. After creating the model, assign the Steel AISI 1020 107 HR material and calculate its mass properties. All dimensions are in mm.

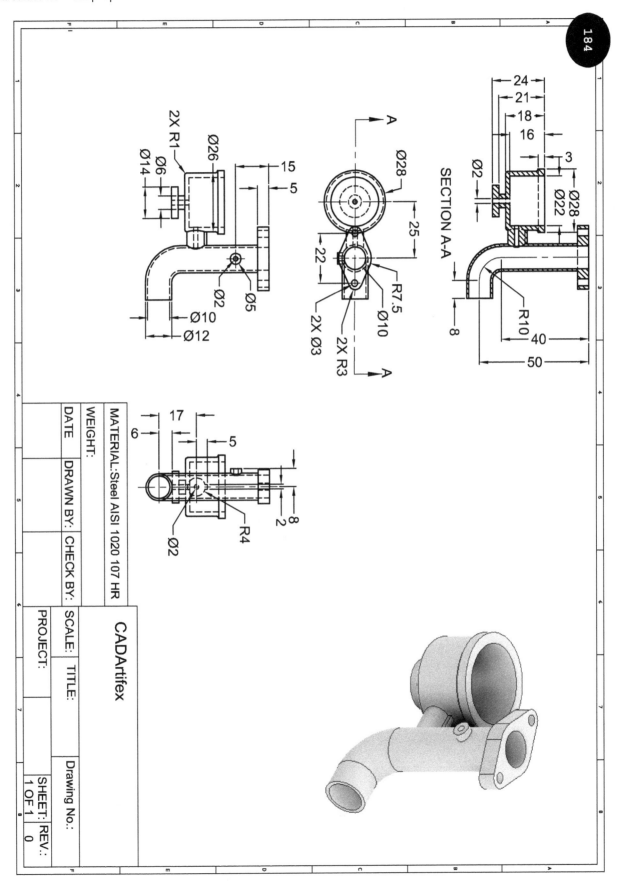

Exercise 99.

Create the 3D model, as shown in Figure 185. Different views of the model and dimensions are shown in Figure 186. After creating the model, assign the Steel, Carbon material and calculate its mass properties. All dimensions are in inches.

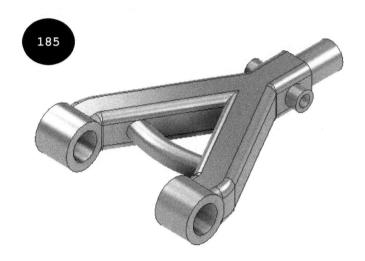

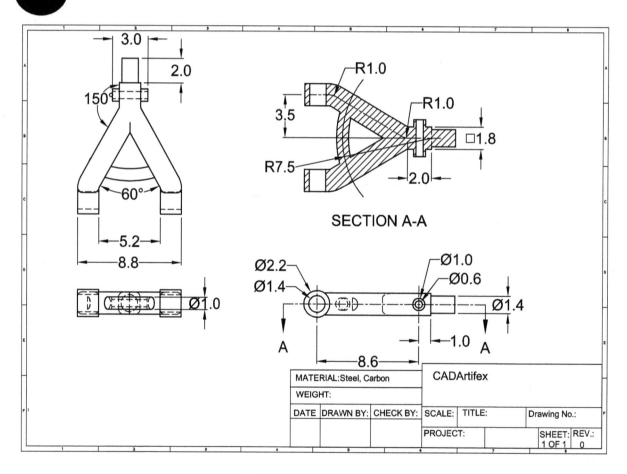

SECTION A-A

MATERIAL:Steel, Carbon			CADArtifex		
WEIGHT:					
DATE	DRAWN BY:	CHECK BY:	SCALE:	TITLE:	Drawing No.:
			PROJECT:		SHEET: 1 OF 1 REV.: 0

Exercise 100.

Create the 3D model, as shown in Figure 187. Different views of the model and dimensions are shown in Figure 188. After creating the model, assign the Steel, Carbon material and calculate its mass properties. All dimensions are in mm.

187

186

Ø80
Ø50

42

4X R8

R20

2X R5

R2 TYP

Ø60

DETAIL VIEW A

80

VIEW A

VIEW B

A

A

45°

45°

B

R50

8

60

40

A

A

15

R50

Ø84

Ø70 Ø60

10

47

8

SECTION A-A

MATERIAL:Steel, Carbon	CADArtifex		
WEIGHT:			
DATE	DRAWN BY:	CHECK BY:	SCALE:	TITLE:	Drawing No.:
			PROJECT:		SHEET: REV.: 1 OF 1 0

Mass Properties in Kilograms of Each Exercise:

Exercise No.	Mass in Kilograms (kg)
1	1.174
2	0.148
3	0.123
4	16.439
5	1.592
6	19.220
7	3.472
8	0.145
9	13.209
10	0.464
11	3.306
12	37.615
13	16.562
14	11.681
15	0.214
16	0.177
17	0.075
18	12.198
19	0.318
20	2.270
21	0.022
22	0.428
23	0.101
24	4.884
25	6.395
26	1.151
27	0.251
28	0.014
29	2.105
30	6.554
31	0.610
32	2.110
33	0.304

34	31.795
35	0.145
36	1.351
37	0.654
38	1.734
39	0.223
40	3.981
41	1.494
42	1.257
43	158.148
44	21.554
45	7.167
46	0.777
47	0.968
48	71.374
49	0.287
50	0.226
51	3.648
52	0.801
53	0.299
54	0.815
55	14.537
56	0.831
57	1.725
58	1.847
59	5.005
60	3.864
61	0.189
62	5.707
63	15.250
64	2.202
65	0.025
66	0.136
67	18.739
68	20.710
69	0.286

70	1.351
71	16.990
72	2.228
73	2.617
74	8.527
75	18.357
76	11.122
77	10.890
78	120.137
79	0.125
80	0.406
81	0.309
82	15.728
83	0.600
84	1.123
85	2.201
86	0.863
87	40.035
88	56.957
89	3.822
90	5.506
91	8.163
92	6.743
93	15.735
94	509.076
95	430.743
96	59.739
97	16.734
98	0.059
99	8.160
100	2.738

Other Publications by CADArtifex

Some of the other Publications by CADArtifex are given below:

AutoCAD Textbooks

AutoCAD 2024: A Power Guide for Beginners and Intermediate Users
AutoCAD 2023: A Power Guide for Beginners and Intermediate Users
AutoCAD 2022: A Power Guide for Beginners and Intermediate Users
AutoCAD 2021: A Power Guide for Beginners and Intermediate Users
AutoCAD 2020: A Power Guide for Beginners and Intermediate Users
AutoCAD 2019: A Power Guide for Beginners and Intermediate Users
AutoCAD 2018: A Power Guide for Beginners and Intermediate Users
AutoCAD 2017: A Power Guide for Beginners and Intermediate Users
AutoCAD 2016: A Power Guide for Beginners and Intermediate Users

AutoCAD For Architectural Design Textbooks

AutoCAD 2023 for Architectural Design: A Power Guide for Beginners and Intermediate Users
AutoCAD 2022 for Architectural Design: A Power Guide for Beginners and Intermediate Users
AutoCAD 2021 for Architectural Design: A Power Guide for Beginners and Intermediate Users
AutoCAD 2020 for Architectural Design: A Power Guide for Beginners and Intermediate Users
AutoCAD 2019 for Architectural Design: A Power Guide for Beginners and Intermediate Users

Autodesk Fusion 360 Textbooks

Autodesk Fusion 360: A Power Guide for Beginners and Intermediate Users (6th Edition)
Autodesk Fusion 360: A Power Guide for Beginners and Intermediate Users (5th Edition)
Autodesk Fusion 360: A Power Guide for Beginners and Intermediate Users (4th Edition)
Autodesk Fusion 360: A Power Guide for Beginners and Intermediate Users (3rd Edition)
Autodesk Fusion 360: A Power Guide for Beginners and Intermediate Users (2nd Edition)
Autodesk Fusion 360: A Power Guide for Beginners and Intermediate Users

Autodesk Fusion 360 Surface and T-Spline Textbooks

Autodesk Fusion 360 Surface Design and Sculpting with T-Spline Surfaces (6th Edition)
Autodesk Fusion 360 Surface Design and Sculpting with T-Spline Surfaces (5th Edition)
Autodesk Fusion 360: Introduction to Surface and T-Spline Modeling

Autodesk Inventor Textbooks

Autodesk Inventor 2024: A Power Guide for Beginners and Intermediate Users
Autodesk Inventor 2023: A Power Guide for Beginners and Intermediate Users
Autodesk Inventor 2022: A Power Guide for Beginners and Intermediate Users
Autodesk Inventor 2021: A Power Guide for Beginners and Intermediate Users
Autodesk Inventor 2020: A Power Guide for Beginners and Intermediate Users

FreeCAD Textbooks

FreeCAD 0.20: A Power Guide for Beginners and Intermediate Users

PTC Creo Parametric Textbooks

Creo Parametric 9.0: A Power Guide for Beginners and Intermediate Users
Creo Parametric 8.0: A Power Guide for Beginners and Intermediate Users
Creo Parametric 7.0: A Power Guide for Beginners and Intermediate Users
Creo Parametric 6.0: A Power Guide for Beginners and Intermediate Users
Creo Parametric 5.0: A Power Guide for Beginners and Intermediate Users

SOLIDWORKS Textbooks

SOLIDWORKS 2023: A Power Guide for Beginners and Intermediate User
SOLIDWORKS 2021: A Power Guide for Beginners and Intermediate User
SOLIDWORKS 2020: A Power Guide for Beginners and Intermediate User
SOLIDWORKS 2019: A Power Guide for Beginners and Intermediate User
SOLIDWORKS 2018: A Power Guide for Beginners and Intermediate User
SOLIDWORKS 2017: A Power Guide for Beginners and Intermediate User
SOLIDWORKS 2016: A Power Guide for Beginners and Intermediate User
SOLIDWORKS 2015: A Power Guide for Beginners and Intermediate User

SOLIDWORKS Sheet Metal and Surface Design Textbooks

SOLIDWORKS Sheet Metal and Surface Design 2023
SOLIDWORKS Sheet Metal Design 2022
SOLIDWORKS Surface Design 2021 for Beginners and Intermediate Users

SOLIDWORKS Simulation Textbooks

SOLIDWORKS Simulation 2023: A Power Guide for Beginners and Intermediate User
SOLIDWORKS Simulation 2022: A Power Guide for Beginners and Intermediate User
SOLIDWORKS Simulation 2021: A Power Guide for Beginners and Intermediate User
SOLIDWORKS Simulation 2020: A Power Guide for Beginners and Intermediate User
SOLIDWORKS Simulation 2019: A Power Guide for Beginners and Intermediate User
SOLIDWORKS Simulation 2018: A Power Guide for Beginners and Intermediate User

Exercises Books

Some of the exercises books are given below:

AutoCAD Exercises Books

100 AutoCAD Exercises - Learn by Practicing (2 Edition)
100 AutoCAD Exercises - Learn by Practicing (1 Edition)

Autodesk Inventor Exercises Books

Autodesk Inventor Exercises - Learn by Practicing

SOLIDWORKS Exercises Books

SOLIDWORKS Exercises - Learn by Practicing (3 Edition)
SOLIDWORKS Exercises - Learn by Practicing (2 Edition)